Quarto is the authority on a wide range of topics.

Quarto educates, entertains and enriches the lives of
our readers—enthusiasts and lovers of hands-on living.

www.quartoknows.com

First published in the United States of America in 2015 by
Race Point Publishing, a member of
Quarto Publishing Group USA Inc.
142 West 36th Street, 4th Floor
New York, New York 10018
quartoknows.com

Visit our blogs at quartoknows.com

10 9 8 7 6 5 4 3 2 1

ISBN 978-1-63106-161-5

Library of Congress Cataloging-in-Publication Data is available

Editorial Director: Jeannine Dillon
Managing Editor: Erin Canning
Senior Design Manager: Heidi North
Interior Design: Phil Yarnall / SMAY Design
Cover Design: Phil Yarnall / SMAY Design

Printed in China

Front cover photography © Colin Jones/TopFoto/The Image Works; © Hulton-Deutsch Collection/CORBIS; © Neal Preston/Corbis; © Graham Lowe/Getty Images

Back cover photography © Pictorial Press Ltd./Alamy

See page 224 for a complete listing of the photography credits

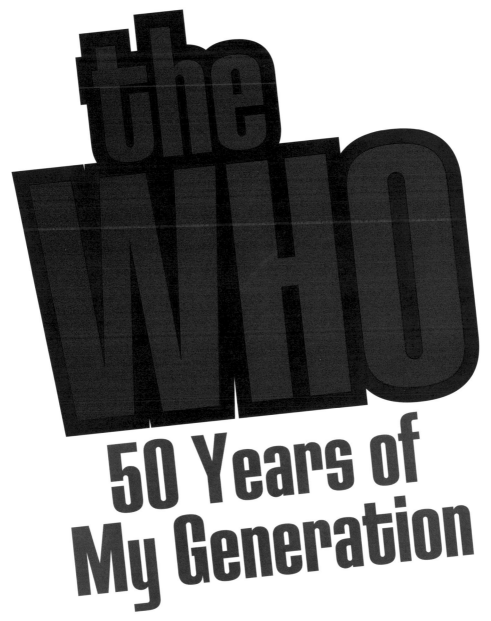

the WHO

50 Years of My Generation

MAT SNOW

Race Point
PUBLISHING

the WHO 50 Years of My Generation

OPPOSITE: The Who when they briefly traded as the High Numbers, summer 1964. From left: Pete Townshend, Roger Daltrey, Keith Moon, and John Entwistle.

introduction

the Who

FIFTY YEARS? Asked to predict the Who's life expectancy, for much of their history many insiders would have reckoned about five minutes.

Band of brothers? Hardly. Close harmony group? You must be joking.

Seldom has a rock band comprised such strikingly different personalities—such temperaments locked in mutual frustration, even outright conflict. Yet it is that conflict that has fueled an intensity of feeling and performance unmatched by any of the other great rock bands that emerged in the '60s.

As musically groundbreaking as the Beatles or Beach Boys? Probably not. As sexy as the Stones? Not really. As epic in sound and spectacle as Led Zeppelin or Pink Floyd? Debatable. But for the full expression of the turbulent inner world of the young guy—and the young guy who still lives inside nearly every old guy—no one beats the Who. And that goes for quite a few girls, too.

Frustration. Idealism. Yearning. Self-questioning. Confession. Black humor. Ambition. Weakness. Rage. Vaulting creation. Shattering destruction. It's a combustible, irreconcilable mixture. Yet what guy has not gone through all these phases— many at the same time? This is what the Who are all about, and why they connect so deeply to so many generations of rock fans.

And it's from their fans that the Who have always drawn their greatest inspiration. One of many London pop/rock bands scuffling on the live circuit that was booming in the wake of Beatlemania and the burgeoning R&B movement spearheaded by the Rolling Stones, the Who found their audience—and their inspiration—when for a few months in 1964 they became the High Numbers, the house band of west London's mod scene, then at its peak. Immersing themselves in the subculture, the four performers formed a two-way bond with their audience—both affectionate and combative—that continued long after mod itself had faded and new subcultures arisen.

LEFT: "Sleeping" it off in Morningside Park, New York City, April 1968.

ABOVE: Pete Townshend on stage in 1965 in his trademark Union Jacket and windmilling his Rickenbacker guitar.

as roundabout, often whimsically oblique self-therapy, Pete formulated the Who's first epic masterpiece, exploring the very idea of followers and leaders, visions and missions, transcendence and spirituality. Thus *Tommy*, the double album that challenged the Beatles' *Sgt. Pepper* at the '60s summit where pop meets art.

But this milestone had by no means exhausted the inspiration of these ideas for Pete. Because it never found a final, overall shape and was never completed, *Lifehouse* was the missing link in Pete's life work, and yet it yielded some of the greatest songs of the Who's career. As far back as 1970 he prophesied the Internet and virtual reality, but a coherent narrative structure eluded him.

Much more concrete was the Who's second fully formed rock masterpiece. Conceived as both a generational and group self-portrait with an eye on the Who's approaching decade, *Quadrophenia* pictured an emblematic mod fan of the Who whose personality has four facets, one representing each member of the band. Such was Pete's approach to understanding the complex chemistry of the group and the scene that had empowered them: poetic, grandiose, psychological, and mythic all at once.

An album whose status has grown to towering proportions over the years, *Quadrophenia* was the culmination of a strenuously explored, mutually passionate, decade-long relationship between four guys up onstage and the thousands of individuals on the other side of the lights.

Where did the Who go from there?

At first downhill. And then in circles.

Yet the bond was now unbreakable, and the

Articulating what the fans themselves could not became the band's mission. The Who's main songwriter, Pete Townshend, decided to get inside their heads and give them a voice—even if it was a stuttering, angry, and thoroughly mixed-up voice. When he wrote "My Generation," Pete became the spokesman for the war and postwar austerity babies coming into adulthood in the brave new world of the 1960s.

It was a tough job, and like one of his main inspirations, Bob Dylan, Pete backed away from articulating issues and instead moved toward articulating feelings. Through two years of songwriting sense of communion when the Who take to the stage has never dimmed. When the Who hit their stride, they split the atom with a charge of energy that lights up every synapse for miles. That remains true in all the decades that have followed their first few, furious years. From contemporaries the Action, to hard rockers Blue Öyster Cult, to punks the Sex Pistols, to stadium world-beaters U2, to grunge rebels Pearl Jam and beyond, up to the present day, the Who remain the inspirational live rock band against whom all others must be measured.

But offstage, after years of fame and fortune had unmoored Pete from the fans, his agonized self-exploration in song was to herald a long aftermath that would reverberate well beyond the Who's explosive first decade.

That aftermath has not been without its own shocks. First came the death of Keith Moon. The Who doggedly carried on—unlike Led Zeppelin, who promptly broke up on the death of their drummer—marking themselves out as pragmatists as well as idealists. They even survived the next trauma, when eleven fans died at a concert in Cincinnati at the very end of the '70s.

Nor did the shocks end when the Who became veterans replaying old glories to both their own generation of old faithfuls and

new generations of the fascinated young. For all the fighting, no one ever quit the Who. Following his buddy Keith twenty-four years later, the contrastingly saturnine mystery man John Entwistle went down the fatal road to excess despite approaching sixty, his final hours spent on cocaine with a groupie in Las Vegas.

Which leaves those old adversaries, Roger Daltrey, who formed and bossed the band until challenged by Pete, the guitarist he recruited and who usurped his leadership through sheer force of creativity. Divided by a gulf in upbringing, temperament, talent, and ambition, they spent years at each other's throats in an atmosphere of mutual incomprehension and suspicion, but came to grudgingly respect what the other could do. Fifty years on, rumor has it they have not only begun to understand each other, but even quite like each other.

The Who: for generation after generation, the ultimate rock band. And this is the book that not only shows but tells it like it was—and is.

ABOVE: The Who trip out during the psychedelic Summer of Love, 1967. Flower power never really suited them.

chapter 1

Blitz Babies

THE WEEK that polio-stricken Irene Daltrey was due to give birth to her first-born, London was under Luftwaffe attack. German bombs hit such landmarks as Horse Guards Parade, St. James' Park, the Treasury, the Admiralty, the War Office, and the Scottish Office, with windows blown out in 10 Downing Street, official residence of the prime minister, Winston Churchill.

That week, some five hundred Londoners were killed, including seventy-two who died after a direct hit on a block of flats in Chelsea, west London. Three years after the far more devastating Blitz, Londoners called the new assault on their city the Baby Blitz. And when, during a rare lull, the overdue Iris was rushed to hospital from the air-raid shelter near her home in west London's working-class Shepherd's Bush, the boy to whom she gave birth fully merited the same name: Baby Blitz.

Just five-foot-six in adulthood, Roger Harry Daltrey was born on March 1, 1944, his insurance clerk father then serving overseas with the Royal Artillery. When that summer the Germans unleashed their secret weapons on London and a V-1 "Doodlebug" destroyed the house next door, Irene fled with baby Roger to a remote Scottish farmhouse, where wartime malnutrition bowed his legs and stunted his growth.

OPPOSITE (clockwise from top left): Roger Daltrey, Pete Townshend, John Entwistle, and Keith Moon.

It was not until he was over a year old that Roger's family was reunited in London, the exhausted adults, like so many others, desperate for the blessings of peace after six years of war. Yet it was precisely their parents' need for a humdrum, untroubled postwar life that was to fuel their offspring's craving for excitement as they grew up among the bombsites of the last war and in the shadow of the annihilating nuclear mushroom cloud of the next. Not for nothing were the children born to the wartime generation called the baby boomers.

Though meriting his later reputation as a hard man with a barely concealed hostility to flashy

ABOVE: Pete (far right), age ten, on holiday in the Isle of Man with his best friend, Graham "Jimpy" Beard, and their mothers.

intellectual endeavor and a soft spot for London's criminal underworld, as a young boy Roger was a bright, well-adjusted all-rounder—a sportsman, a church chorister, a trumpeter in the Christian Boys' Brigade, a violinist, skillful with his hands, and diligent at school. All that changed when he turned eleven, and the Daltreys—now with two daughters as well as Roger—moved from cramped Shepherd's Bush two miles west into the leafy suburbs of Acton, where Roger passed the demanding Eleven Plus exam and entered Acton County Grammar School. There, teachers and other schoolboys made it very clear to Roger that the new kid was not only funny-looking—his chin stuck out after he broke his jaw in an accident—but also came from the wrong side of the tracks. Bullied, sneered at, and told he wasn't good enough, Roger was a fish out of water—and he hated it.

Music in Their Genes

No less a misfit at Acton Country Grammar but hiding it behind a half shell of conformity was John Alec Entwistle. As his name would suggest, he was born of Lancashire stock on his father's side and to musical genes on both sides. Another Hammersmith Hospital baby, John arrived on October 9, 1944, but soon found himself being brought up by his tax office clerk mother back at his maternal grandparents' home near the Daltreys in Acton—his parents' marriage, like so many others, failing to survive the stresses and separations of the war.

Good at art as well as singing, John also took up the trumpet and then the French horn, and like Roger joined the Boys' Brigade as well as precociously making his showbiz debut playing for a local dance band. For John, music offered an escape from a sense of dislocation that came about after his mother remarried and the family moved to where Acton

ABOVE: Cliff Townshend (front row, third from left) performing with the Squadronaires.

abutted the even leafier Ealing. Far more variegated than London's almost solidly working-class East End, the city's sprawl to the west of the center was a patchwork of housing, light industry, and offices, and therefore of numerous gradations of working- and middle-class Londoners at a time of acute class consciousness and snobbery.

Compared to the Daltreys and Entwistles, the Townshends had money. But compared even to the Entwistles, for much of their son Pete's childhood, they were far from a stable family. Father Cliff was a professional musician who in the '30s had flirted with fascism as a British "Black Shirt," but upon World War II's outbreak had joined the Royal Air

Force, where he played clarinet and saxophone in the RAF Dance Orchestra, among whose popular war-time tune was "There's Something in the Air," its title foreshadowing a No. 1 single that his as-yet-unborn son would produce twenty-eight years later.

In 1944, after a whirlwind courtship of only seven consecutive Sundays, Cliff married the Orchestra's new featured singer, Betty, the child of a broken home of singers and performers. On May 19, 1945, with the war in Europe just over, even though Japan remained undefeated for another three months, their first-born Peter Dennis (his maternal grandmother's surname) Blandford (his paternal grandmother's surname) Townshend was born in

ABOVE: A young Pete smiles, but he is nursing secret trauma.

Isleworth, near the fast-growing London Airport at Heathrow. Though he was privately educated since the age of four, the only child Pete grew up in an atmosphere of turbulence at home, with his father frequently away with the band, now renamed in peacetime the Squadronaires (and featuring "Cliff Townshend and his Singing Saxophone"), and mother Betty beginning bitterly to regret that she had married in haste. During school holidays, the family would reunite wherever the Squadronaires' date sheet happened to take them, and young Pete was initiated early into the world of adult glamour, dancing, fun, noise, and alcohol.

It all went wrong for Pete at the age of six. Always flighty, Betty's mother Emma—"Grandma Denny"—had begun to concern her daughter with behavior that verged on the unstable. Believing little Pete would be a calming influence, his parents sent him to live with her over eighty miles away in her small flat in Westgate-on-Sea in Kent. It was a terrible error of judgment. Being that he was only six, Pete's recollection of exactly what happened is sketchy, but it includes frequent and undeserved canings not only at his new elementary school but also by Denny herself, who would also withhold food, scrub him viciously at bath time, and even hold him underwater while he struggled to breathe.

Beyond even this Dickensian treatment, Denny seemed obsessed by the US servicemen at the nearby Manston Air Base, and she would demand little Pete accompany her on walks there at dawn. One of the servicemen persuaded the little boy into his car, at which point, years later, the middle-aged millionaire rock star's recollection of events ended. Strange men were around, and in the flat, too, and whatever happened was more than the six-year-old could process. Pete would repress the memories of these experiences for decades, but they haunted his subconscious and would surface in some of his most celebrated songs. Later still, they would trigger the most profound crisis of his life. Only fleetingly visited by his mother—and hardly at all by his father, who made do by spoiling Pete with money to buy toys—the little boy lived in, as he later admitted, "constant fear."

Then, suddenly, it was all over. Back in London, his mother was having an affair and Pete changed schools yet again. The only anchors in his life were his best friend Graham "Jimpy" Beard and, briefly, a dog called Bruce. Like many showbiz kids—another at the same time being another son of a band musician, John Baldwin, later more famous as John Paul Jones of Led Zeppelin—Pete was never settled enough to form close friendships, so he retreated into himself. To her credit, Denny had forced him to learn to read properly, and Pete was to immerse himself in the world of imagination and fantasy.

As for music, Pete's parents had no desire to nurture their only child into so uncertain and disruptive a profession, and when he was enthralled by the sight and sound of a one-man band playing a harmonica, he felt compelled to steal one, his father refusing to buy him one. Yet music—through the excitement, fun, and allure of the adult world that it sound-tracked—had

Pete in its grip. Pete was in love with the life of Saturday night, which was at its most exciting when, in a step up from the usual summer round of holiday camps, the Squadronaires played the Palace Ballroom in the seaside resort of Douglas on the Isle of Man, which would provide a happier memory that later inspired one of the Who's early hit singles.

Cliff Townshend's parents owned a piano, and his grandparents and Aunt Trilby offered the musical encouragement Pete never got from his dad, though his parents—ever eager to get him out of the house so they could work on their misfiring marriage—did encourage him to go to Sunday school, where not only did Pete develop a religious consciousness but he also found a sense of belonging in the choir.

Mistakenly, he also thought he would find a sense of belonging in the Sea Scouts, a wing of the Scouts (in which the young Keith Richards was an eager member over in Dartford) that kept lads off the streets and out of trouble by allowing them to muck about in boats. According to his recollections—which contract, expand, and change according to his mood—Pete was to experience the first of a number of transcendent moments on the river when, blending with a motorboat's outboard engine, he heard the sound of angels singing—an auditory vision of overwhelming intensity echoing that of the great London poet and artist William Blake who had seen angels some two centuries before. But while he was never to return to the Sea Scouts, Pete would return to boats and the water, forever associating them with a mood of transcendent purity as summoned by the voices of angels.

Not that the sound that would change everything the year Pete went to Acton Country Grammar was ever likened to the voices of angels.

chapter 2

Year Zero!

FOR GENERATIONS of kids all over the world, 1956 was Year Zero. It was the year rock 'n' roll became the sound of teenage life—a movement rather than a one-off. The one-off, who was to be swept aside by the deluge he unleashed, was an avuncular cow-licked trouper called Bill Haley, whose band, the Comets, had stripped down and speeded up western swing dance music to create a hit sensation on both sides of the Atlantic the year before with "Rock Around the Clock." Rock 'n' roll was a novelty with an edge of teenage delinquent threat, having been enthusiastically adopted by "greasers" in the United States and "teddy boys" in the UK, but for a while it might have seemed like another dancehall craze that would come and go.

Then, in early 1956, came Elvis: a teenage pinup and role model in a way that the too-old Haley never could be. Elvis Presley had hit after hit, and then came the movies, and then came still more rock 'n' roll stars, each with something different and no less exciting to offer. If Elvis had the sneer and pelvis on which he'd swing his guitar, Jerry Lee Lewis and Little Richard were men possessed by hellfire lust on the piano. Then came the songwriting brilliance of singing guitarists Chuck Berry and Eddie Cochran, while Buddy Holly, with his Crickets, and Gene Vincent, with his Blue Caps, created the backing group as team and gang, respectively.

LEFT: Teens excitedly gather outside a cinema showing the movie *Rock Around the Clock*, 1956.

There is probably not a single British rock legend of the '60s who was not fundamentally and profoundly inspired by some or all the American rock legends of the '50s, who also included Larry Williams, Fats Domino, Johnny Burnette, Link Wray, the Everly Brothers, all the doo-wop groups . . . the list goes on.

Pete was a Haley devotee, and he thought Elvis "a chump," but Roger was smitten. For Roger, disaffected at school, and legions of patronized working-class kids like him, Elvis was another kid from the wrong side of the tracks who triumphed in style, making the conventional idea of a successful young man look soft, square, and boring. Roger wanted some of that—and school could take a running jump.

"I wanted to be Elvis Presley when I grew up," said Roger years later. "But the man who really made me feel like I could actually go out and do it was a chap by the name of Lonnie Donegan."

Rock 'n' roll was harder to play than it looked, and to get a good sound you needed real instruments. Proper electric guitars and amplifiers made by the likes of Fender and Gretsch were expensive imports from America. Fortunately, right on cue came a parallel new music that anyone could have a go at playing; rock 'n' roll you could make yourself from the cheapest ingredients: skiffle.

Cheap, Cheerful, and British: Skiffle!

Britain had a long-established homegrown jazz scene, and by the mid-1950s a revival of the earliest recorded jazz style—small-group traditional ("trad") Dixieland, as spearheaded in New Orleans by the likes of Louis Armstrong in the early '20s—was well underway. Lonnie Donegan was a sideman banjoist who became a star when his interval "skiffle" shows within a show—where he played American folk and blues tunes by Woody Guthrie and Lead Belly on a cheap guitar, a bass made from a tea chest, and a washboard as percussion—took off with audiences. His version of Lead Belly's "Rock Island Line" was a huge hit in 1956, and within months, it is said, some thirty thousand schoolboy skiffle groups had formed in Britain. From the Beatles to the Stones, Led Zeppelin to Pink Floyd, this is where it all started.

Making his own guitar, Roger formed the Sulgrave Rebels with friends at the Sulgrave Boys' Club in his old neighborhood of Shepherd's Bush, won a local contest with homemade instruments, and promptly broke up the band. Roger had discovered girls and had no time for music. School was out, too, after he was expelled at age fifteen for smoking—the culmination of numerous infractions relating to his teddy-boy hair, loud clothes, and surly attitude.

Driven less by role models than by music itself, John formed a band at school that was a notch up from skiffle. Though he was not particularly a fan of Dixieland jazz, it was—unlike rock 'n' roll—a style of music with trumpet at its heart and a strong grassroots audience, especially in west London. John's trad group, the Confederates, needed a banjo player, and it just so happened there was a new boy at Acton Country Grammar who had struggled with guitar and so taken up the banjo, playing it with a bright, slashing aggression. Looking to escape a house now filled with a crying baby since the birth of his brother Paul, Pete Townshend—his outsize nose as much the object of derision at his new school as Roger's jaw—wanted to join a gang to give him a positive identity.

With Pete not being interested in team sports, that gang would be musical; and with him being from a jazz background through his parents and sharing John's sense of humor, which ran from *Mad* magazine to *The Goon Show* with Peter Sellers and Spike Milligan, the older boy's group, the Confederates, was a perfect fit.

For a while the band held together, but soon rock 'n' roll began to exert its magnetic pull, dragging Pete and John away from trad jazz toward the guitar-based music of Duane Eddy (whose twanging lead lines and chugging rhythms would be a huge influence on John), the Everly Brothers, and Rick Nelson, with the clean-cut but musically credible British act Cliff Richard and the Shadows proving to these schoolboys that you didn't need even to be American to make good, tuneful, homegrown rock 'n' roll. Pete had bought a cheap guitar from his mother's new business, an antique and bric-a-brac shop, to which he attached a pickup, and then acquired an amp. John, having toyed briefly with guitar, added bass to his repertoire of instruments, making his own and painting it mauve. Renaming themselves the Aristocrats and then the Scorpions, the band played Shadows covers in youth clubs and other small gatherings of music fans in the local area.

Just as there was an explosion of young, skiffle-inspired bands, so there was a corresponding explosion in demand. Teenagers wanted to dance to music of their own rather than the show-band music of their older siblings and parents, and the idea of dancing to records rather than a live act was still years away. And it was all about dancing, face-to-face and with as much sexiness as the average repressed British teenager on the cusp of the '6os could summon. From the jive to the stroll to the world-conquering twist, then the mashed potato,

the monster mash, the monkey, the dog, and the frug, new dance styles arrived from the United States every year, adopted, adapted, and added to in London and all over Britain.

The keenest dancers were beginning to coalesce into a self-conscious youth tribe. Calling themselves "Modernists," they worshipped the snappy elegance of modern jazz musicians like Miles Davis and lived for the weekend, when they would display the latest dance moves, as inspired by the hottest soul, jazz, and rhythm-and-blues records while wearing the latest clothes—preferably bespoke tailoring based on the most elegant new fashions from Italy, France, and the United States. It was a highly competitive scene, ranked according to arcane codes of coolness. The mod scene would grow in the course of the early '6os to play a crucial part in the story of the Who.

Meet the Detours!

For now, stylistic elegance was a long way away for John, Pete, and Roger. In his first job, the former grammar school boy, whose education and parents' aspirations had directed him toward white-collar work, had progressed from electrician's mate to apprentice sheet-metal worker, making his hands a mess of cuts that frustrated his renewed ambition to be a rock 'n' roll musician playing a self-made electric guitar (or, in his dreams, an imported Fender Stratocaster like the Shadows' Hank Marvin).

Invited to join a local rock 'n' roll covers band, Roger leaped at the chance with an audition performance of Elvis' "Heartbreak Hotel," but it was as much his confidence and focus that got him in the band. In short, he had what any band needed to stay together, rehearse, develop, perform, and improve: self-discipline and leadership qualities.

Among his first acts as the effective leader of the band he had just joined was to name them—after the Duane Eddy hit "Detour," they would be the Detours. He also started getting them gigs, so when the band's bassist left to take up a better offer, he was able in turn to tempt the talented brass and bass player he knew from his old school to quit his schoolboy band for a going concern. When, a little later, the Detours needed another guitarist, John was able to recommend his old Confederates mate. Recalling Pete as "a nose on a stick" in the year below at school, Roger sounded him out. Wary but impressed by Roger's aggressive personal style, Pete was up for the challenge.

It was the start of 1962. Roger Daltrey had recruited local school-leavers John Entwistle—who had followed his mother into clerical work at the local tax office—and Pete Townshend to join the scuffling rock 'n' roll band he led. They had cheap and improvised equipment and rehearsed, mostly in Roger's house when his parents were out, far more often than they performed—and, when they did, it was for meager sums like £7 (around nineteen dollars at the time), split six ways. All over Britain, boys were joining bands that scratched out versions of American rock hits for their friends and whatever paying audience they could find. Nor were the Detours uncommon in incorporating other styles and songs into their repertoire based on the instruments they had on hand, which in this case meant trad jazz numbers with Roger on trombone, John on trumpet, and Pete on banjo.

Most of these thousands of scuffling young bands would come and go without making much impression. But of the young British would-be rockers who did make an impression, many had one curious thing in common: art. While Roger toiled away by day as a metalworker and dreamed of being a musician by night, Pete had no such focus. Neither committed to following in his father's footsteps as a professional musician nor sure of what else he wanted to do except be creative, Pete was off to art school.

ABOVE: The Detours play in January 1963, just as Beatlemania is about to sweep Britain and revolutionize the music scene.

chapter 3

Artist, Teddy Boy, Taxman . . . and Maniac!

FOR BRITISH BOYS born during World War II, there came a dramatic moment when they hit age eighteen. For years, British males could expect to be "called up" to do national service in the armed forces. But from the late '50s on, in the teeth of anxiety that without the discipline of a spell in uniform British youth would degenerate into a hooligan rabble, national service was abolished. Better yet, educational opportunities were opening up for those about to leave school. Among them, for creative types who were not necessarily academic, were art schools.

At worst, these new art students would lounge around as trainee Bohemians; at best, they would be inspired by a whole new universe of creative ideas and people. Among Britain's war-baby future rock stars who went to art school were the Beatles' John Lennon; the Rolling Stones' Charlie Watts, Keith Richards, and Ronnie Wood; guitar gods Eric Clapton, Jeff Beck, and Jimmy Page; the Kinks' Ray Davies; and Pink Floyd's Syd Barrett. The world of art may be the poorer for their not following up on their studies professionally, but the world of music is immeasurably richer.

LEFT: Pete, artist and Bohemian, reading D.H. Lawrence's cause célèbre novel, *Lady Chatterley's Lover*, banned for obscenity for forty years in Britain, but a best seller once legalized.

Next door to the Townshends lived the cartoonist Alex Graham, whose comic strip character, Fred Basset, remains a fixture in the *Daily Mail* to this day. Alex liked Pete's drawings and encouraged him to try his luck at the nearby Ealing Art College. Aged sixteen, Pete got in, and just so happened to find himself there at a pivotal moment in the college's history when training students to be commercial draftsmen was on the way out, and New York's hip, free-form, no-rules conceptual art had captured the curriculum of the foundation course. Creative and mental liberation was top of the teaching agenda, and most influential on Pete was Gustav Metzger, a Jewish refugee from Nazi Germany whose installations and performance art, which involved using breaking glass and acid as mediums, were all about destruction. Auto-destructive art was new and exciting, and in the era of the 1962 Cuban Missile Crisis—when Pete, like so many others, feared nuclear obliteration—it spoke to the moment.

Pete led an increasingly Bohemian life with a measure of independence, where he could broaden his musical taste with modern jazz and rhythm-and-blues records. The wry grooves of Jimmy Reed and Mose Allison were among his favorites—the former, along with John Lee Hooker and Hubert Sumlin, feeding into a guitar style that was diversifying from its basis in jazz, the Shadows' Hank Marvin, and country picker Chet Atkins. This side of his life he kept quiet from his fellow Detours. To Pete, they were a party band playing country-and-western and whatever was in the pop charts—a nice little earner, but hardly an outlet for his burgeoning sense of being a creative person, aside from his creating a band logo painted on the side of their van, to which he added an arrow to the "o" of "Detours," a visual pun combining a road sign indicating an upcoming detour and the symbol for male. It was an idea Pete has seen used by the British pop artist Peter Blake (who, in 1967, would create the legendary cover for the Beatles' *Sgt. Pepper* album), and it was not the last time he would be inspired by him.

ABOVE: Back at the start in 1964 at Shepherd's Bush Bingo Hall, London.

ABOVE: Keith Richards of the Rolling Stones in 1963, an early influence on Pete.

The Beat Explosion

Beatlemania gripped Britain in 1963, and bands who could sing, play, and look good were in huge demand as the nation's teens hit the clubs and halls, enjoying the moment with all its excitement and craving for new groups and new sounds.

As spring bloomed into summer, the Detours were filling their engagement diary and earning ever-larger fees on London's expanding live music circuit thanks to their varied repertoire, growing professionalism, and gig-booking connections made through Pete's parents. Yet the guitarist felt his future lay with kinetic art rather than a band he considered too corny and uncool to tell his art school friends about. But when he wrote a Merseybeat-style song and had it accepted by a music publisher, he decided to use that prestige and his added value to the band as an original songwriter to push them in the cool direction he wanted. Musically, that would be a blend of

the Memphis-made organ-versus-electric-guitar soul instrumental "Green Onions" by Booker T. & the MGs and the hard, chopping four-piece rock 'n' roll of one of the few truly great pre-Beatles British rock bands, Johnny Kidd & the Pirates, whose 1960 hit "Shakin' All Over" would later enter the Who's live repertoire.

Though it rankled Roger that the band's musical direction was being set by an art school layabout who on more than one occasion had to be dragged out of bed in a cannabis fog to get to the gig on time, by the fall of 1963 he noted that while they were losing their old audience for Beatles-lite renditions of pop hits, they were gaining a bigger one as London's live rhythm-and-blues boom gathered mass and momentum. When the Detours supported the up-and-coming Rolling Stones that December, Pete was smitten by their sound, style, and charisma.

Seeing guitarist Keith Richards raise his arm to crash down on a chord, Pete was bewitched. After being assured that Keith was just limbering up rather than striking a dramatic pose, which it would be uncool to copy, Pete adopted the "windmill" slash at the guitar as his own. With both arms aloft as his guitar fed back howls of noise through the evermore powerful amplification that he and John were buying from west London's leading musical equipment specialist, Jim Marshall, Pete was nicknamed "the Birdman" by the band's growing coterie of rhythm-and-blues-loving fans, many of whom were mods.

So Nearly . . . the Hair!

To continue the upward curve of their gigging career, the Detours needed to get a record out as both a calling card and a sign that they were in the same league as other emerging London rhythm-and-blues bands like the Rolling Stones, the Yardbirds, and the soon-to-be-renamed Kinks. When they discovered that there was a recording act called Johnny Devlin & the Detours, they realized they needed a new name, too. The Hair was considered—Beatles-style over-collar hair was all the rage for boys who dared risk the wrath of their elders. But when Pete's roommate and partner in both weed and lounging about, Richard Barnes, suggested the Who—enigmatic and short, which meant that each letter would print up impressively big on gig posters—so hungry was bandleader Roger to quit his sheet-metal job and make a real go of music that he set aside reservations of a further encroachment on his turf by the group's arty wing and decided to go with it.

Things were moving fast for the newly christened Who, to whose "o" on the logo was added the Detours' old arrow. Like so many other groups of the day, they handed over their management to people with no relevant experience but money to invest in this glamorous youth explosion. Helmut Gorden manufactured doorknobs in Shepherd's Bush and fancied his chances as the new Brian Epstein. Through a connection of drummer Doug Sandom, the Who were then auditioned by an A&R man for the Fontana label. This ended up rebounding on Doug because the A&R man did not rate him as a drummer, being that he was a traditional timekeeper rather than a player who drove the beat. He was also a decade older than the rest of the band, and his wife resented the time he spent gigging away from home. In short, the rest of the band decided that Doug had to go. Loyal John had misgivings but would never resist a majority consensus. Doug was ousted, and Pete has wrestled with guilt ever since he learned that, the year before, Doug had defended him to the others when, unbeknown to him, his own position was under threat for not looking the part of a handsome rock guitarist.

So, in April 1964, the Who began auditioning drummers. As soon as they heard him not only handle the tricky R&B rhythm of Bo Diddley's "Roadrunner" but also half wreck the kit with the force of his playing,

they knew that in a baby-faced seventeen-year-old "gingerbread man" dressed entirely in orange-brown—with hair dyed to match—they had even more than they had bargained for: a cocky, confident, charismatic sticks man who could beat all-comers for excitement and dynamism.

Keith John Moon had been born to motor mechanic Alf and cleaner Kitty in Park Royal, northwest London, on August 23, 1946. If ever there was a real-life Bart Simpson, it was Keith. The class clown par excellence, he put all of his considerable energy at school into pranks, his hyperactivity working through bugle and trumpet in the local Sea Cadets until he found his ideal mode of expression: something he could hit.

When he joined the Who, Moon had owned a drum kit for only a year. But tutored by Carlo Little of proto-shock-rockers Screaming Lord Sutch & the Savages (who was shocked into agreeing to teach the cocky kid because no one previously had summoned up the nerve to ask him), he made blitzkrieg progress and gigged for a number of semi-amateur west-London bands, notably the Beachcombers, London devotees of California's cultish surf sound spearheaded by Jan & Dean and the Beach Boys, unlikely but enduring favorites of a force-of-nature sticks man in the jazz-avalanche style of Elvin Jones.

So then there were four: Roger, a former teddy boy ambitious enough to see rhythm and blues as the future of any group serious about success; Pete, a gangling, extravagantly nosed art student with lofty aspirations and lazy lifestyle; John, the musically gifted, security-seeking, and secretive child of a single parent; and Keith, the manic, cocky trickster who sounded like no other drummer on the circuit.

None of them were mods. But that is precisely what they would agree to be molded into in their next move.

chapter 4

Mods!

BY THE SPRING of 1964, the mod army had gained mainstream notoriety for fighting at seaside resorts with rival gangs of would-be Marlon Brandos, or "rockers," who remained loyally attached to the motorcycles, leather, and rock 'n' roll of the '50s.

Thanks to the Beatles, followed by the Stones, the Pretty Things, and others, long hair was coming in for young men; mods, however, wore theirs short but assiduously styled and attended to with a steel comb without which no mod would leave home. Mods were like peacocks, the male being far more attentive to ever-changing sartorial detail than his girlfriend, spending a fortune on sharp London tailoring in Italian, French, and American styles, which would often discreetly upstage that of his boss in the office, where he would work to earn the money to spend on clothes and weekend-long, amphetamine-sustained dance parties to which he would travel on his nippy Italian scooter, customized with light-catching rearview mirrors, protected from the elements by a US Army–style surplus-store fishtail parka.

LEFT: Mods, dedicated followers of fashion, out window-shopping.

RIGHT: The Scene club in London was a mod hub where the Who were regulars in late 1964.

Musically, mods also favored the imported over the homegrown. They loved the latest American soul and R&B records, and Jamaican ska, and would check out live bands who played in those styles, notably Georgie Fame & the Blue Flames, resident at Soho's Flamingo Club, a mod hub along with the Scene.

From Vespa to Lambretta, Fred Perry to Levi's, Tamla Motown to Blue Beat, mods were label-obsessed consumers decades before the mainstream, and as well as being a subculture, they were also a market. Such was the insight of Peter Meaden, a twenty-two-year-old hustler who had cut his publicist teeth assisting another young hustler, Andrew Loog Oldham, image-maker and manager of the Rolling Stones. For £50 (around $140 at the time), this colorful Soho character promised the Who a complete makeover to corner the mod market. This seemingly well-connected and hotwired personality seemed to capture the moment, and both the band—especially pop art fan Pete, who was fascinated by the idea of blending creativity and commerce—and their manager, Helmut Gorden, bought into his vision and expertise. What they did not know was that Meaden was a pill-dealing guzzler of Drinamyls (amphetamines blended with barbiturates to take the edge off, given the street name "purple hearts"), who had a score to settle with Oldham, with the Who his intended vehicle to prove he could better his old boss in transforming an interesting new band into a headline-news hit act.

Haircuts came first, and then a fashion make-over, with singer Roger dressed in an Ivy League seersucker jacket while the instrumentalists looked boyish in boxing boots and skating jackets. More tellingly came yet another name change. The Who were now the High Numbers—"numbers" being just above "tickets" but below "faces" in the mod pecking order, and "high" a wink to their target market's fondness for an array of "uppers" or "leapers" to fuel all-night dancing, and for pot and "downers" to return them to earth, ready for work on Monday.

Though Pete was now a published songwriter, Meaden demanded control of the High Numbers' first single, released on the Fontana label, which cloned the Dynamics' "Misery" for its A-side, "Zoot Suit," and Slim Harpo's "I Got Love if You Want It" for its B-side, "I'm the Face." Fontana was unimpressed, however, and failed to promote a pressing of only a thousand copies. The band's hardcore

following aside, most mods saw through the opportunism and were not buying it, while Fontana did not exercise its option for a follow-up. The High Numbers had flopped, and the four were shocked at just how badly Meaden's persuasive master plan had failed.

At this critical moment when, disheartened, the band might have broken up and Pete returned to art school, the cavalry rode to their aid.

Enter Lambert and Stamp

With Beatlemania spearheading an explosion in pop music and teenage culture, mid-'60s London bristled with opportunists eager to shape and invest in young talent, in return to reap the rewards when mania came their way too. Kit Lambert, twenty-eight, and Chris Stamp, just turning twenty-two, were two such opportunists, yet were so much more.

It is hard to imagine a less likely partnership. Kit (Christopher) was the upper-bracket son of the famed composer, ballet conductor, and music critic Constant Lambert, a bon viveur and swain of prima ballerina Margot Fonteyn, whose vision of integrating jazz with classical music was snubbed by the British musical establishment, and who died frustrated. Gay and rudderless but immensely charming and resourceful, Kit was an ex-army officer and failed Amazon explorer with a score to settle with the establishment on his late father's behalf.

Chris, meanwhile, was the no less good-looking brother of the fast-rising Cockney heartthrob actor Terence Stamp. A ladies' man where Kit favored male "rough trade," Chris was style-obsessed, and though he had connections with London's East End underworld, he wanted to make it in the movies, and had talked himself into various jobs in Britain's

OPPOSITE: The Who, like the Stones, projected sullen rebellion.

movie industry, itself then undergoing a minor creative and commercial boom. In 1963, on the set of *The L-Shaped Room*, he ran into Kit, who was also successfully hustling various jobs on the fringes of the movie industry, and the pair struck up a business partnership based on the shared idea of making a gritty, realistic movie about a real pop group that would clean up at the box office. It was a great idea, and the Beatles' *A Hard Day's Night* would do just that in summer '64, just as the High Numbers were failing to capitalize on mod-mania.

Kit had been systematic in scouring London for the band he needed to fit the bill, and eventually he found them that July, playing in Harrow at the Railway Hotel pub, into which he'd been drawn by the swarm of scooters parked outside. Having introduced himself to comanager Meaden, Kit got the hard sell, which confirmed his belief based on what he saw onstage and the crowd's reaction to it that this was the band he was looking for. Summoned from a location shoot in Ireland, Chris Stamp saw them too, and he agreed. Without giving up on the movie idea, the pair's ambition expanded to taking over the band's management—which, of course, required not only the band's consent but also the removal of Helmut Gorden and Peter Meaden.

The Takeover

Getting the band's consent was not automatic. They liked Meaden, but they had worked out that not only had he no money and quite a pill habit, his response to the failure of his mod makeover was to redouble his efforts in the same direction. Just as bold in their bluff and promises but much less twitchy, Lambert and Stamp not only offered to match the £20 weekly wage Gorden was paying each of the four musicians, but bet a further £120 that they could get the group a Top 20 hit.

Believing the posh Kit to be wealthy—in fact, he had to sell a family heirloom to bankroll the band's wages—the four musicians decided to take the pair's offer. The way was smoothed when it was found that Pete's parents had cannily neglected to counter-sign the band's management contract when he was legally underage, so rendering it invalid. Meaden, meanwhile, was paid off with £500 in cash.

The deal that Lambert and Stamp agreed with the band was a six-way earnings split, with the notable exception—at the insistence of his parents, who struck out that clause from the contract—of Pete's songwriting publishing earnings. Though a mere detail in August 1964, this would become a huge issue over time, as Pete got into his stride as a songwriter: not only would he create most of the band's material but, as a result, he would earn a great deal more money than the other three. Roger was the founder of the group and by far its most focused and determined member, but his leadership had to be continuously asserted in the face of his arty layabout guitarist's creative talent.

Troublesome in a different way was that Roger was being pressured to live a lie: that he was not, in fact, married. Teenage girls drove record sales, and they liked their pop stars single and hypothetically available—the latter of which certainly applied to the relentlessly philandering Roger, but the former did not, since not only had he married Jacqueline Rickman the year before but they had just produced a baby, Simon. But just as Roger was hungry for the fringe benefits of being a pop singer, his determination to make the band succeed was unwavering.

Still calling themselves the High Numbers, the four continued to work on their live act, building their support and venturing beyond their west London stronghold. Kit and Chris had not forgotten their original idea to make a movie, so they shot footage of the band onstage in Harrow's Railway Hotel, performing mod-friendly songs by Smokey Robinson & the Miracles, Howlin' Wolf, and Jessie Hill. Pete is twitchy, angular, and strange, his moves almost from the school of minimalist modern dance, while Roger, short and dressed for August in summer clothes, has an air of menace behind his shades. Yet upstaging them both is Keith—manic and flailing, like no drummer before him. Word of mouth drew the curious as well as the committed over the course of the rest of the year, with Tuesday nights at the Railway Hotel being where the band felt most at home.

The band were working on flashing stage lights and other attention-grabbers when they played big halls, as they did just a week after that filmed Railway Hotel show on a bill at Blackpool's Opera House, below the Kinks and untouchable headliners the Beatles. A bit older than the High Numbers, the Beatles needed no light show nor even to perform audibly, drowned out as they were by their screaming, pants-wetting fans. As for the Kinks—four-piece rock rivals from north London—they were ahead of the west Londoners, too: streaking up the charts to No. 1, their song "You Really Got Me" delivered precisely the forceful, moody menace on record that Roger, Pete, John, and Keith were honing on stage. The four realized how far they had to go.

When the breakthrough came, it was literal. Overnight, it became the band's gimmick, what made them stand out, and what came to define them—especially when art student Pete began weaving theory into practice . . .

Auto-destruction!

RIGHT: Pete poses with his Rickenbacker 345.

chapter 5

Smash It Up!

THE BLACK-AND-WHITE FOOTAGE of the band playing Harrow's Railway Hotel in August 1964 confirms what everyone who was there says about the birth of British rock: it was really a very small, accessible scene. Until they started having hits and graduating to the theaters, future legends like the Beatles, the Stones, Eric Clapton, and Rod Stewart played pubs and clubs with no physical or emotional distance between the musicians and the audience at all. Everyone was on the same level—sometimes literally.

To be seen from the back, of course, an act needed a stage, and often boards placed on beer crates did the job. The High Numbers decided to invest in something better: a portable collapsible stage. The first time they erected it at the Railway Hotel, probably one Tuesday that September, all went well until Pete started throwing his "Birdman" shapes, which were building into quite a repertoire of exciting moves made all the more dramatic for Pete being so tall and thin. At a crucial moment in a song, Pete would thrust his Rickenbacker electric guitar upright and upward, but had not calculated that the new stage raised the band higher than before, and his guitar head smashed through the low ceiling.

When a posse of Ealing Art College girls in the audience started sniggering, Pete who had only lost his virginity the year before and, with his nose and gawkiness, was sensitive about looking a fool in front of girls—lost his temper and completely smashed the guitar, for which he'd still not fully paid off the installment plan. Feeling very much better in the process, he then calmly strapped on his spare Rickenbacker twelve-string and carried on as if nothing had happened. The fans, of course, were stunned; afterward, the thrifty Roger was not happy.

LEFT: By 1967, the Who turned on-stage auto-destruction into a fine art.

The following Tuesday at the Railway Hotel, the crowd was agog with expectation: would he do it again? The contrary Pete didn't oblige but Keith did, kicking over his kit at the end of the set. Again, the fans reacted with delighted shock. Such calculated destruction of equipment that cost months of wages was daring and confrontational. One week later, both Pete and Keith trashed their instruments, and the High Numbers had a unique, compelling act. Soon even Roger joined in, whirling his microphone lead like a lasso, the mic smashing into Keith's cymbals.

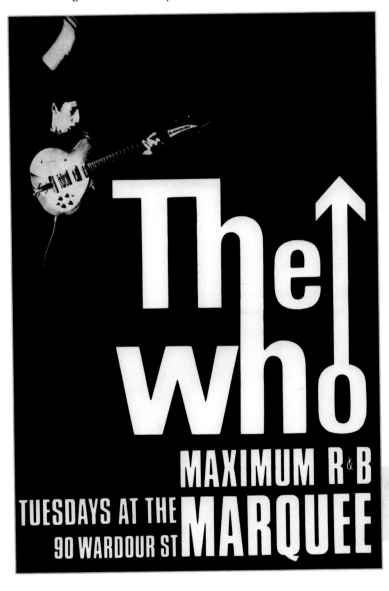

Maximum R&B!

Kit Lambert loved the rebelliousness—even nihilism—of this developing act, and was fascinated by the way band and fans formed a bond of cliquish aggression. The former artillery officer formulated a plan to mobilize the mod fans as word-of-mouth marketers of the band like guerilla insurgents.

Pete, having now decided not to return to art school, was bringing his art-school thinking to the band instead and beginning to justify the group's stage act along the lines of Gustav Metzger's symbolically loaded auto-destruction. Kit, who saw the High Numbers as his vehicle to shock and mock the establishment that had rejected his father's progressive musical ideas, was ready to bankroll the band, who were now trashing more than they were earning, though cannily the three (never John, unflappably static within the chaos) became careful to try not to shatter instruments beyond repair.

In the fall, the Railway Hotel banned the group for some forgotten infraction, but luckily Tuesday nights became available in Soho's Marquee Club. To fill this central London venue, the group mobilized their fan base and created an iconic black-and-white poster of Pete "windmilling" his guitar above the words "MAXIMUM R&B: TUESDAYS AT THE MARQUEE, 90 WARDOUR STREET." Alongside that, of course, was the name of the band: the Who, with the male arrow jutting defiantly from the "o."

LEFT: The poster announcing the Who's residency at the Marquee Club.
OPPOSITE: Pete solders a repair to a Fender Telecaster scratch-plate; smashed guitars were patched up and reentered into the fray.

By reverting to their earlier name, the band now had the graphic impact to match their stage impact—and maximum impact from minimal means was what the mods were all about. After a slow start, said mods began to flock to the Marquee, from the Who's first show there, on November 24, 1964, into New Year 1965. The Who played twenty-two consecutive Tuesdays, and such was their wall of noise, as provided by state-of-the-art Marshall amps, and the band's heedless auto-destruction, particularly when Kit had spotted media people in the increasingly packed crowds, that by spring not only were the Who the most talked-about band on the live circuit but the Marquee—hitherto a shabby jazz club—had been firmly put on the map as one of London's leading live rhythm-and-blues venues.

A crucial milestone in the Who's rise to fame (or notoriety) came in 1965 with their first single under their proper name, and their first recorded number written by Pete: "I Can't Explain." Obsessed by the fear that the Kinks had stolen a march on the Who with their No. 1 single "You Really Got Me" and its even tougher follow-up, "All Day and All of the Night," in late '64 Pete worried away at a similarly tough, riff-driven song, testing it out on friends in the soundproofed ad-hoc demo studio he had converted from a bedroom in his parents' house. He also worried away at lyrics, keen to express his insecurities and those he detected behind the self-confidence of the Who's young mod audience but fearful that the cocky, aggressive Roger would dislike or fail to deliver convincingly that kind of song. Not for the last time, Pete underestimated Roger's ability to get into character—to portray feelings he would never have himself, or at least would never admit to having.

LEFT: Playing one of their talked-about shows at the Marquee Club.

Happy at last with his song, "I Can't Explain," Pete had no qualms when, through a friend of the band, they contacted the groundbreaking producer of the Kinks' hits in the hope he would be interested in trying to repeat the magic. Aged twenty-seven, Shel Talmy had come over from California in 1963 with clear and tested ideas about how to record rock acts in the studio for maximum impact on disc at a time when most British record producers had little clue. He liked the Who and the song, and he heard commercial potential.

With his track record as a hit producer, Talmy was able to dictate his terms. And having no better immediate options, the band and management accepted his offer: the Who would sign exclusively to Talmy's production company for five years in return not only for financing and producing their records but also for working his record industry contacts to get the group

a deal. With the exception of Keith, Talmy failed to get on with the band, and fell out badly with Kit, who imagined, like Andrew Loog Oldham with the Rolling Stones, that he should have a hands-on role in the recording studio with his band.

Even so, Talmy delivered a great-sounding record in "I Can't Explain," different than the Kinks' dirty, overdriven sound in its ringing clangor. Supported by Keith's love of vocal harmony groups like the Beach Boys, Talmy also called in the Ivy League to provide better backing vocals than he thought the Who could sing themselves. Ace session man Jimmy Page, later a founder of Led Zeppelin, was also called in, but his guitar part is inaudible in the final record. As for a deal, Talmy called in a favor with Decca Records in the United States, which owned the Brunswick label in the UK, hence "I Can't Explain" being released in the United States a few weeks before its UK release on January 15, 1965.

ABOVE: The Who's debut single, "I Can't Explain."

RIGHT: The band in the fall of 1965 post their success with "I Can't Explain" and their residency at the Marquee Club.

ABOVE: At the *Ready Steady Go!* studio, 1966.

BELOW: From 1966, their *Ready Steady Who* four-track EP.

Ready Steady . . .

Though the debut single by the totally unknown Who
barely scraped into the US Hot 100, in the UK it began
to climb the charts, hugely helped by a lucky break
when not only were the Who booked to perform on
British TV's most popular yet also hippest music show
but they were able to pack the audience with mod fans
of the bands waving that week's fashion must-have,
the college scarf. *Ready Steady Go!* was broadcast
on British commercial TV on Friday evenings and
showcased live in a dynamic club setting both such
homegrown stars as the Beatles, the Rolling Stones,
Dusty Springfield, and the Dave Clark Five—and such
visiting Americans as the Supremes, Stevie Wonder,
the Beach Boys, James Brown, and Marvin Gaye.

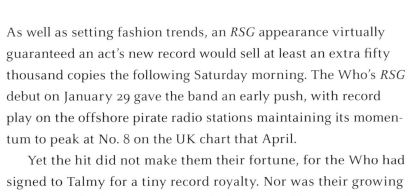

As well as setting fashion trends, an *RSG* appearance virtually guaranteed an act's new record would sell at least an extra fifty thousand copies the following Saturday morning. The Who's *RSG* debut on January 29 gave the band an early push, with record play on the offshore pirate radio stations maintaining its momentum to peak at No. 8 on the UK chart that April.

Yet the hit did not make them their fortune, for the Who had signed to Talmy for a tiny record royalty. Nor was their growing success on the live circuit—on which they could now charge a fee of £300 a night—making money, either. So colossal were the costs of auto-destruction that, despite their rising fame, both band and management were sinking deeper into debt, which was sustained by Kit Lambert's luck at the gaming tables and perceived creditworthiness as an upper-crust gentleman residing at smart addresses. Chris Stamp's salary from working as an assistant director on the shoot for the Kirk Douglas war movie *The Heroes of Telemark* helped with cash flow.

For a little while the money problems did not seem to matter. The Who were now on the cusp of becoming a nationwide sensation.

ABOVE: Keith upstages Roger—literally. The two would clash.

RIGHT: Performing "Substitute" on Ready Steady Go!

chapter 6

Breakthrough!

IF YOU SAW THE WHO PLAY one of those legendary Marquee shows, you heard some very cool songs chosen to hit the mod target, performed with swagger and the cliff-edge excitement of unpredictability. During that breakthrough to a national profile, for their live set the Who relied on songs by the cream of America's rhythm-and-blues and soul artists: James Brown, Marvin Gaye, Smokey Robinson, Martha & the Vandellas, Howlin' Wolf, Bo Diddley, Mose Allison, Chris Kenner, Phil Upchurch, and many more.

Roger remembers singing those songs with particular fondness; perhaps tellingly, none of them were by Pete. Could the budding songwriter repeat the success of "I Can't Explain"? For the Who to prosper, he would have to. Even though the band had recorded numbers from their live set that April for a first album which, like the hit debuts by the Rolling Stones and even the Beatles, was proposed by their record company to consist heavily of covers, the game had changed even since those albums released in '64 and '63. In writing their own terrific songs, the Beatles had set the bar for any rock group who wanted to be taken seriously—and, through song publishing royalties, make real money. The Rolling Stones' manager, Andrew Loog Oldham, knew this, and had locked Mick Jagger and Keith Richards in a kitchen until they had written a song, and now their writing partnership was beginning to bear fruit in the early-'65 hit single "The Last Time," with the band's anthem, "(I Can't Get No) Satisfaction," to come that summer. The Kinks' Ray Davies, meanwhile, was writing hit after hit, each more daring than the last. And in America, Bob Dylan and the Beach Boys' Brian Wilson were writing songs that extended the spirit of friendly competition across the Atlantic, the former's originality and genius as a lyricist inspiring Pete as well as every other aspiring songwriter of

LEFT: The Who are ready to become an original songwriting band.

ABOVE: Miming to your hit was standard '60s practice on television.

the day.

Kit Lambert suspected that Pete had what it took to join the songwriting elite and decided to hothouse his talent by moving him in to share his flat in Swinging London's swanky Belgravia and giving him a musical education in the classics, from his own father's work and his British contemporary William Walton through the baroque composers Corelli and Henry Purcell (a lasting Pete favorite), in particular his suite "The Gordian Knot Unty'd." Removed from the dope-smoking comfort zone of sharing a place with his buddy Richard Barnes in suburban Ealing, the lapsed

art student was bought state-of-the-art tape recorders—like John Lennon, Pete early adopted the idea of experimenting and making demos in a home studio— to help him flex his creative muscles. An affair with Kit's assistant Anya Butler, ten years older than the guitarist, further boosted his confidence.

Dead for a decade, bebop jazz giant Charlie Parker was not an obvious inspirational figure for a rocker. His parents' musical background aside, Pete could not help but drink in a live jazz scene that overlapped with London's rock and R&B scenes (the following year, the Who would face their first serious challenge for onstage volume and power from Cream, formed when two jazzmen joined forces with R&B guitarist Eric Clapton). The wild sense of freedom of Parker's saxophone inspired Pete's follow-up to "I Can't Explain." "Anyway, Anyhow, Anywhere" was an anthem of boundlessly self-confident possibility, and even more so when Roger tweaked the lyrics to reflect his tough, punchy personality. Though less catchy than its predecessor, the Who's second single was wilder and more representative of their stage act, featuring not only Keith's drums, which were miked for even more impact, but also what was then the most radical guitar solo in rock's short history—a blaze of dive-bombing glissandi, calculated amplifier feedback, and Morse code bleeps as Pete toggled between his guitar's bridge and neck pickups. (Decca's pressing plant engineers thought the recording was faulty until it was explained it was meant to sound like that.)

The Art of Confrontation

Though a slightly smaller hit than the first single when released that May, "Anyway, Anyhow, Anywhere" made more of a statement about the Who. Band and management were now presenting an image beyond mod to embody all of pop art itself. As much as this was a bold, inventive,

TOP: The Who's second single, "Anyway, Anyhow, Anywhere."
ABOVE: In early 1966, the Who seethed with discontent.

ABOVE: Influenced by British pop artist Peter Blake, the Who put their own spin onto the mod look.

and novel idea, it also was economically necessary at a time when Kit was struggling to stay one jump ahead of the bailiffs as the Who's debt mounted. Mod fashions were expensive, and though the band borrowed most of the latest clothes they wore for photo shoots, their new direction was cheaper but more flamboyant: over a decade before punk, they customized their clothes with medals, military ephemera, the national flag—including Union Jack jackets—and eye-catching graphics inspired by the pop art paintings of the British Peter Blake and American Jasper Johns and the op-art works of London's Bridget Riley. No one else was doing this, and the striking style started a fashion for vintage military uniform that peaked with the Beatles' *Sgt. Pepper* album cover two years later.

Never one for style for its own sake, Pete proclaimed in the press that everything the Who did was to mock and deny convention and tradition. But Roger was chafing. The time was right to record and release a debut album, and the singer thought it should contain plenty of the soul and blues covers that the Who played live to reflect their show, the appeal of which was going from strength to strength, in London and beyond. But Pete was going for all-out originality, which meant writing as many songs as he could. The more conservative Roger was not convinced this would be as commercial.

And then there was the growing tension between Roger and Keith. The drummer's manic showmanship and mugging at the audience behind Roger's back irritated the upstaged singer. Nor did Keith's manner help. Impressed by Kit's louche, top-drawer self-confidence, Keith mimicked his manager's upper-crust style, morphing in less than a year from working-class London lad to theatrically grand champagne-quaffer and a pill-popper on a growing scale. A habitué of Swinging London's booming after-hours clubs like the Scotch of St. James, the drummer who would sooner have been a singer like his beloved Beach Boys and Beatles befriended Ringo Starr and Paul McCartney, his zaniness endearing him as court jester to the crowned heads of pop. The Beatles became fans as well as friends, with Paul telling the press, "The Who are the most exciting thing around."

Keith's fellow carouser and closest buddy in a band of men who all lived in each other's pockets during years of endless gigging was the quiet one, John. An odd combination of fearless extrovert and cautious near-introvert, he and Keith shared a sense of humor and fondness for bubbly and pharmaceuticals that propelled the taker in "an upward direction, dear boy," to quote the man soon to be known as Moon the Loon. Roger, meanwhile, had to look after his voice, so he kept the drink and drugs to a minimum. Self-denying (apart from sexually) and in a hurry, he was annoyed by the others' self-indulgence—and in Keith's case, scene-stealing, and, in Pete's, time-wasting pretension.

But Kit was backing Pete.

All-Out War

The original movie idea had slipped down the managers' agenda, with Kit in particular increasingly seeing the Who as an art project to thumb one's nose at an establishment that had rejected his father's bolder visions. And when Pete had his eccentric choice of car—a 1935 Packard hearse—towed away by the police on the orders, so goes the guitarist's story, of the Queen Mother, who objected to seeing this reminder of the funeral of her late husband years before on her drive to Buckingham Palace, it inspired the band's next move.

Outraged by such abuse of *lèse-majesté* and what it said about the privileges of class and age, Pete fell to work on a protest song in the

wry, talking-blues vein of Mose Allison, Jimmy Reed, and Bob Dylan—its sound like mid-tempo Bo Diddley. Demo followed demo, each version heeding Kit's encouragement to make it harder, more radical, more confrontational. But the final "Anyway, Anyhow, Anywhere" retained a lot of the original idea's hipness and humor, from the soulful handclaps to the placement of a bass solo where you would expect a guitar solo. Later, in the studio, tempers frayed, with John frustrated in his attempts at trying to capture the twangy sound he wanted with various combinations of instrument and strings. The key tension, though, remained between Roger and everyone else, and it all boiled over that September.

First, while the Who's roadies were parked outside a London dog rescue center, looking over a German Shepherd to guard the equipment, their van was broken into—and loads of equipment stolen. A few weeks later, the Who were in Holland, playing on borrowed equipment and not happy with the sound. Worse followed in Denmark, when—playing very badly thanks to drink and amphetamines but blaming their substandard borrowed gear—Pete, Keith, and John provoked the audience's 4,000 drunken young farmers to riot before a single song had been completed, making headlines in the next day's Danish papers.

Backstage in the dressing room, a furious Roger, feeling frustrated and let down by his bandmates, got into an ugly fight with Keith after flushing his stash of "French blues" down the toilet. Finally fed up with Roger's physical threats and tendency to turn to abuse to win an argument, the other three turned on him. Roger was out—fired . . . but then provisionally reinstated after three days. The band's workload was too heavy to do without him in the short term, and in turn the band was Roger's

Two weeks later, against this background of an uneasy truce, the Who went into the studio with Shel Talmy and recording engineer Glyn Johns, on his way to becoming one of rock music's premier producers. There, over two days on Tuesday and Wednesday, October 12 and 13, at IBC Studios in London, the Who cut the tracks that would complete a classic album, including the one that would not only title that album but also become the single that would define the band forever. Over a decade before punk, this new rock anthem would thrill the young and rebellious and confront the establishment with a surly, mocking, and violent challenge to the old order: "My Generation."

ABOVE: Keith's increased drinking and drug use was becoming worrisome.

RIGHT: The Who's anthem, "My Generation."

life—almost literally. No longer at home with his wife and child, he lived in the band's furniture truck, which got them from gig to gig. He promised to moderate his behavior while they got on with their commitments of not only an exhausting date diary, with shows ever further from London as they expanded their fan base, but the recording of a debut album and a new single.

Peace was restored—for a while.

chapter 7

Pop Art Stars!

"MY GENERATION" was literally an overnight sensation, recorded as Wednesday, October 13, 1965, faded into Thursday morning, when the Who had to be out of the studio. Pete had worked on his demos, and with each review his mentor Kit encouraged him to turn it up; make it more confrontational, more of a statement in word and sound. Consisting of just two verses, repeated, with the refrain "Talkin' 'bout my generation," one phrase in particular hit its target: "I hope I die before I get old." Then there was the stutter. An old bluesmen's trick used sometimes for comic effect, here Pete had Roger go into character as the "amphetamine-blocked," tongue-tied mod given a voice. No one had heard anything like it.

Where pop's bad boys, the Rolling Stones, were clearly a threat to the moral welfare of the nation's teenage girls, the Who took rebellion to a whole new level: if you were old, they despised you. Even their music mocked the idea of order and decorum; based on a heavy descending riff played in unison on electric guitar and bass, the song's handclap rhythm was thrillingly disrupted by Keith's drums exploding over the beat. With its instrumental break played by John on the bass—seldom if ever a soloing instrument before now— the whole song broke down in a freak-out of drums and feedback guitar. You could picture Pete and Keith smashing their gear, as indeed they did when the song ended their live show.

LEFT: The Who rock *Ready Steady Go!*

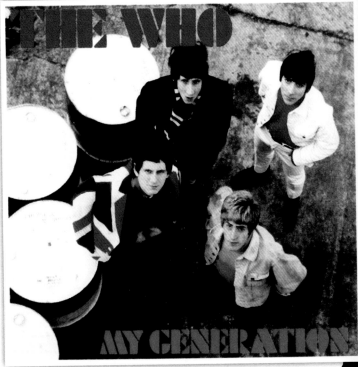

Released only a fortnight after it was recorded, the single proceeded to sell 300,000 copies to reach No. 2 in the UK chart, held off the top only by the Seekers' folk-pop weepie "The Carnival Is Over." The Who's notoriety had spread far beyond pop fans. Arrogant and thuggish yet clearly calculated in what they did and said—and how they looked, sounded, and presented themselves—they were the new public enemy number one for everyone who thought the country was going to the dogs.

Also titled *My Generation*, the Who's debut album was released on December 2 for the lucrative Christmas market, though most stockings that year bulged with the *Sound of Music* soundtrack or the Beatles' *Rubber Soul.* Hardly festive, the album retained two James Brown numbers and one by Bo Diddley but otherwise showcased Pete as a songwriter who wanted to articulate what he saw a mass of insecurities behind the male mod mask—fear of

ABOVE: The *My Generation* album—a classic the Who almost disowned.

RIGHT: Pete stabs his Stratocaster into a wall of amps at the Marquee Club.

being found out, of losing love, of not being good enough or cool enough. "The Kids Are Alright" poignantly transcended the mod scene (which the Who were edging away from, being as it was both restrictive and also losing its chic thanks to catching on as a mainstream teen fad) to capture mixed feelings of romantic unworthiness and group loyalty. A thrilling instrumental counterbalance, "The Ox," was a group composition turbo-charging a surf favorite of Keith's from 1963, "Waikiki Run" by the Surfaris, where Pete's raunchy guitar riffed and snarled over Keith's revved-up drums while session pianist Nicky Hopkins (soon to be a fixture on some of the very best British rock records) tinkled over the top as if accompanying a saloon-bar brawl in a western.

My Generation is a thrill from start to finish, and, despite being kept off the top by two Beatles albums and two soundtracks for movie musicals starring Julie Andrews, reached the UK Top 5. Yet the Who practically disowned it from the moment of its release. The band were overworked and feeling it, with Keith in particular having to

miss a number of shows. There was a truce but no real rapprochement between Roger and the other three, while Pete and Kit formed an alliance from which the rhythm section felt excluded too.

One thing united them. They all detested Shel Talmy, which soured what they felt about their own recordings. And they blamed him and their record company, US Decca/Brunswick, for failing to get behind their records in the huge American market, which over the previous two years had been hungry for the next big thing from Britain but had not taken the Who's bait at all.

But how to get out of the production and record deal into which they were locked? A bold step was needed. With promoter Robert Stigwood ready to step in with his new label Reaction in the UK and the legendary Ahmet Ertegün's Atlantic/Atco label promising huge backing in the United States—while also offering a very good royalty rate plus a cash advance that would wipe out a lot of debt—the Who and their management decided, after being given legal advice that their Talmy/Decca contract might not be airtight, to break it.

ABOVE and ABOVE RIGHT: Two tracks from *My Generation* spun off as singles, despite the band's objections.

OPPOSITE: Keith and John, buddies, take light refreshment—a rare no-alcohol occasion in 1966.

The Secret Super Group

This they did with "Substitute," a new song by Pete, who also produced the recording of it on February 12, 1966, released three weeks later on the Reaction label. The music for its verses more than inspired by "Where Is My Girl," an unsuccessful single by British pop-rockers Robb Storme & the Whispers, the lyric readdressing with greater wit the anxiety first heard on the *My Generation* album track "It's Not True" about being found out as a fake. Catchy, funny, and far less confrontational than their previous single, "Substitute" gave the Who another Top 5 hit, despite Talmy forcing the withdrawal from sale of the first pressing for infringement of his production style on the B-side and Brunswick trying to kill it with the rival release as a single of

the amusingly apposite *My Generation* album track "A Legal Matter."

Writs flew, and for months the Who were effectively halted in their tracks as recording artists while the dispute was fought. At such a crucial stage in building the group, losing momentum at a time when pop fans expected three singles and two albums a year from their favorite artists could have been fatal to their prospects. They were also forced to rely almost entirely on the live circuit for income, having also, thanks to some murky disagreement with Kit Lambert, lost the offer of a cameo in Michelangelo Antonioni's Swinging London movie *Blow Up*, with the role of the guitar-smashing band going instead to the Yardbirds with Jeff Beck.

The pressure and uncertainty was taking its toll on four young guys who were volatile at the calmest of times. Suffering most was Keith, not yet twenty and soon to be married to pregnant girlfriend Kim Kerrigan—a crisis which so intensified his pill-popping and drunkenness that he had no recollection of playing on "Substitute" and even haplessly tried to gas himself.

Pete, meanwhile, was clearly considering his options, his song publishing income setting him apart from the other three, who would be reduced to pilfering from the door take of that night's show to get by. His songwriting ambitions now extending to screen soundtracks, he was by no means convinced he needed to be in the Who, though he certainly enjoyed live performance and showmanship as his self-confidence grew.

In such an atmosphere of insecurity, bickering, and strain, Keith was tempted to explore his own options, and in May 1966 was flattered to be invited to play incognito with Yardbirds guitarists Jeff Beck and Jimmy Page, the ace session man who had played on "I Can't Explain," now recording for a Beck solo side project. Arriving at the studio disguised in a Russian fur hat, Keith joined Beck and Page plus John Paul Jones on bass and Nicky Hopkins on piano on the super-session that yielded the amazing instrumental "Beck's Bolero."

A new band combining the "Beck's Bolero"

ABOVE: Pete restrings his Rickenbacker, as his penchant for showmanship grows stronger.
OPPOSITE: The Who's contemporaries the Yardbirds, with Jeff Beck (far left) and Jimmy Page (second from right).

talents was mooted, with its members to include a hardly less insecure John, who nearly quit the Who to join the Moody Blues. The band was to be called Lead Zeppelin, after John's joke about how well they were likely to go down with the public; Keith came up with the sleeve image of the dirigible falling in flames. These were ideas that two years later the pair would mention while chatting to a former roadie, Richard Coles, who passed them on to his new boss—Jimmy Page, who was putting a new band together and needed a name.

The Who, meanwhile, were fighting and falling out like never before, with Keith quitting for a week after sustaining a broken ankle and a black eye in a difference of opinion with Pete after a show on May 20, only to return eight days later with a new kit boasting twin bass drums—his signature thereafter.

While the band remained at bursting point, crashing from crisis to crisis, the lawyers and managers were busy cooking a deal to resolve the record and production contract problem, it being in nobody's interest that such a hot property should not be selling records for anybody. What was eventually agreed was a deal whereby Talmy was paid off with a percentage of the Who's future record royalties, Decca U.S. retained the band on an improved deal in the United States, and the German giant Polydor, investing heavily to break into teen-targeted pop music, got them for the rest of the world.

Opera and America: The Future Beckons

With the deadlock broken, the Who were free to record again. Six months after "Substitute," their new single, "I'm a Boy," marked a bold departure in Pete's songwriting, his obsession with fakery spilling into gender confusion with its confession of a boy brought up by his mother as a girl, part of a larger project he had in mind that was set in 1999 and called *Quads.* Though Pete denied at the time any deeper significance, hindsight suggests a ghost of what happened to him as a child with grandmother Denny floating to the surface. Yet the effect is comic—and its charm helped the single to No. 2 in the UK, matching the success of "My Generation." The song's tempo changes and Beach Boys–style feminine harmonies suggested that Pete was not merely keeping up with the growing

TOP: Pete and Keith with manager Kit Lambert.

ABOVE: The single "I'm a Boy" on the Reaction label.

LEFT: John practices the Melodica al fresco, 1967.

formal sophistication of such peers as the Beatles and the Kinks' Ray Davies but that—thanks to Kit introducing him to opera—he was now toying with its techniques as a means to tell a story and switch personas within songs.

This would flower more fully in a nine-minute number the Who recorded for their second album. This album was the fruit of a publishing deal that secured all the band members much needed advance money if they could each pen at least two songs. Roger came up short, so Pete's so-called mini-opera, "A Quick One, While He's Away," filled the gap. Again whimsical in its telling of a tale of sexual infidelity and exploitation, and comic in delivery, it delved into a place whose darkness would become clearer decades later.

More straightforwardly funny was one of John's contributions, "Boris the Spider," penned in a hurry after a drunken nightclub chat he'd had with Rolling Stones' Charlie Watts and Bill Wyman. John sang the vocal in basso profondo, which became his signature cameo and defined his public image thereafter within a band that was turning away from its original R&B and proto-punk tough, arty guitar-rock into something more varied, comic, parodic, and macabre—while still retaining the rock base for the stage. Of Pete's songs, "So Sad About Us" was both a poignant, tuneful album highlight and a throwback to the "Kids Are Alright" style that was strongly influenced by latter-day Everly Brothers, whose "Man with the Money" was a mainstay of the band's live set.

Like "I'm a Boy," the album was produced by Kit Lambert, whose freewheeling, fun-focused motivational skills came as a pleasurable relief to the band after their spell with the technocratic Talmy. On one of Keith's two numbers, "Cobwebs and Strange," the son of classical composer Constant

conducted, while Pete played the penny whistle, John the French horn, Roger the trombone, and Keith the tuba, all of them reverting to their schoolboy selves.

After the band junked the working title *Jigsaw Puzzle*, the Who's second album—named *A Quick One* after the mini-opera and presenting the group in Carnaby Street pop-art style on the sleeve by Swinging London graphic artist du jour Alan Aldridge—came out in December 1966, just in time for Christmas, and almost a year after *My Generation*, and reached one spot higher in the UK album charts. At the same time, the Who released a new single that was not on the UK album but gave its title to the US version, "Happy Jack." A second slice of "I'm a Boy"–style catchy but offbeat pop, it lacked deeper shadows, whimsically summoning a popular figure of fun from Pete's childhood days on the Isle of Man. Peaking at No. 3, it maintained the Who's hot streak in the UK and even crept into the US Top 30—the band's first sniff of longed-for success in the promised land.

ABOVE: The Who performing the single "Happy Jack" on television in 1967.

BELOW LEFT and RIGHT: Pete and John recording their parts for "Don't Look Away."

OPPOSITE: The Who's second album, *A Quick One*, released in 1966.

That summer, Pete had flown to New York to meet the notorious '60s pop wheeler-dealer Allen Klein, who was offering to help the band in the United States. "The first kid I met was at the airport, a little girl, thirteen years old," Pete told the author years later. "She came running up and said, 'I've been waiting here for an English pop group. Are you any good?' I said yes, and she said, 'Good, I'm going to be your fan!' I said, 'Why aren't you at school?' And she said, 'Because I'm Jewish. We can make up holidays. I just tell the teacher it's Chanujanuchanuhah and we're not allowed to eat meat or go to school or study . . .' So that was my introduction to New York, and there was a kind of thrill, but I also thought, these guys are just weird! That girl is probably still a fan of the group today!"

ABOVE: The 1966 single "Happy Jack."

RIGHT: Despite their often serious appearance, the Who also goofed about at times.

chapter 8

Far Out!

FINALLY, AFTER A YEAR OF STRESS and infighting, all looked good for the Who. But success brings challenges, and new acts were after some of their action, taking things to new, far-out extremes. Meanwhile, the amphetamines that fueled the band's fans and sound were fading from fashion, and a drug new to the scene was all the rage: LSD. As 1967 dawned, the game was changing fast. Could the Who stay ahead?

Trends that had been bubbling under in 1966 now came right to the surface of youth culture in the UK and America. Whereas drugs had been long been part of the musicians' world, with its punishing schedules and problems relaxing after the adrenalin of performance, by 1967 the controversy over LSD had made the debate national news. Jazz was all very well because its fans were older, but pop fans were young—were they not being unduly influenced to take drugs by decadent, older pop idols? And was it not so that the drug everyone was talking about, LSD, induced colorful visionary hallucinations of the kind the young would love? And was not marijuana a gateway to the world of far more pernicious drugs, which would cut young people off from reality, make them rebel, and damage their mental and even physical health?

LEFT: Keith and John rock the fairground bumper cars. Seaside shows remained on the gig list as psychedelia dawned.

To an extent, these popular parental fears were well founded, but rebellion became a self-fulfilling prophecy when pop stars became victims of official propaganda and persecution, starting that February with the Rolling Stones. In a raid on Rolling Stones' Keith Richards' country home (while the Who's *A Quick One* and Dylan's *Blonde on Blonde* played on his stereo), organized by the police in cahoots with a muckraking Sunday newspaper—and even, there is now evidence, secret services on both sides of the Atlantic—Keith and Mick Jagger were arrested and charged with possession of illegal narcotics. The battle lines were drawn, and the Who knew which side they were on.

Though John and particularly Keith were keen pill-heads and drinkers, Pete was the one who saw drugs as a window to creativity. A dope smoker in his art school days, the man who had heard angelic music as a boy was intrigued by the visionary quality of the LSD trip. At the same time, he had a new job to do: to scout far-out talent for Track Records, the label set up by Kit Lambert and Chris Stamp with the proceeds of the new deal with Polydor, which would distribute its releases. Pete began to haunt London's new generation of underground psychedelic clubs in the search of talent. A young band from Cambridge called Pink Floyd obsessed him; their light show and freeform guitar feedback was taking the Who's stagecraft to a trippy new place. But they had already signed to the Beatles' company, EMI, so Pete instead signed to Track a crazed singer called Arthur Brown. The following year he would score a massive hit single at a time when the Who were slipping from the charts.

ABOVE: Pete rocks the double-necked Gibson as light shows add to rock's spectacle in 1967.

OPPOSITE: Pete receiving visions near London's Battersea Power Station.

The irony of the Who being upstaged by their own ally would come very soon. Kit and Chris had already signed to Track an American electric guitar ace who had arrived in London that September of 1966 and within weeks had created a sensation in London's music scene with his prowess, inventiveness, and wild, sensual act: Jimi Hendrix. He upstaged everybody, including London's resident guitar gods Eric Clapton, Jeff Beck, Jimmy Page—and Pete, too. Jimi even had a Moon-like drummer, Mitch Mitchell, and massive Marshall amplification. Jimi set out to steal the Who's thunder, and Pete would be troubled by a rivalry between the two men—a rivalry made all the more pointed for the praise that Kit and Chris showered upon the new contender they called "the black Bob Dylan."

Pete and Eric Clapton, meanwhile, would form a close friendship, but Eric's new group, Cream, also signed to Reaction, played improvisational blues-rock with a power and intensity to rival the Who. Hendrix and Cream were heavy, and while the Who still played loud and smashed their gear, their pop songs about donkeys on the beach in the Isle of Man suddenly seemed lightweight. Nor, despite its commercial success and the fun the Who had making it, could *A Quick One* compare to peak albums of 1966 like the Beatles' *Revolver*, Dylan's *Blonde on Blonde*, the Beach Boys' *Pet Sounds*, soul star Otis Redding's *Otis Blue*, or even the Stones' *Aftermath*. And rumor had it that the Beatles were locked in Abbey Road studio creating a new long-playing magnum opus that would amaze the world. The album era was here, and though hit singles still mattered, they were no longer pop's most important money-spinners and artistic statements.

LEFT: On location near London's Tower Bridge on March 18, 1966, miming for Dick Clark's ABC TV show *Where The Action Is*!

Uncle Sam, Jimi, and Lily

On the underground scene in his new psychedelic finery with his girlfriend Karen—the daughter of screen theme and soundtrack composer Edwin Astley—Pete was having a great time. But as rock got heavier, more formally ambitious, and became angled toward older listeners rather than teenage girls, would the Who be left behind?

It was an issue the group put on hold when, that March, they finally touched down for their first shows in the United States, booked by Frank Barsalona of Premier Talent, a key ally in the band's bid to break America. The Who were part of a package that included Simon & Garfunkel, Wilson Pickett, Mitch Ryder, the Blue Magoos, and Cream, promoted by DJ and self-styled Fifth Beatle Murray "The K" Kaufman to play five sets a day, starting at 10:15 a.m., for nine days at the RKO Radio Theater. Though attendances weren't great and there were rows over the running order, the

Who played up their advance reputation for all they were worth, with Pete regularly trashing his guitar while clad in a flashing, fairy light–festooned jacket plugged into the power supply. They made an impact, got plenty of media attention, and returned home far better known in the United States than when they arrived.

Upon returning to the UK, the Who made straight for the studio with barely a moment to decompress in order to record a new single, their first for Track Records. The A-side was titled "Pictures of Lily," with Pete again drawing on the box of camp curiosities that had supplied the band's previous two singles and was very much in the air, from Swinging London boutiques like I Was Lord Kitchener's Valet and the *Avengers* TV show to the Victoriana of the Beatles' forthcoming album. Inspired by a vintage postcard of the legendary music hall star Lily Langtry that Karen had given Pete, it was a tale of boyish insomnia overcome by the companionship and (so many concluded) sexual stimulation of her comely image. Funny, tuneful, and very well performed, especially its vocal harmonies, it was the best of the trio of Who singles from a whimsically youthful perspective. It again made the Top 5 in the UK but no more than brushed the US chart. Tellingly, though, it fared no better than the very first Track Records release, "Purple Haze," by the Jimi Hendrix Experience, a guitar-rock classic that snarled, shrieked, and purred in an ecstasy of flip but calculated menace. By comparison, the Who sounded almost genteel.

LEFT: The 1967 single "Pictures of Lily."

RIGHT: Keith, as precise as he was reckless, on drums.

Pete's sense of being outgunned and threatened with dethronement by his own labelmate would reach its climax two months later. The Monterey County Fairgrounds in Monterey, California, had hosted folk and jazz festivals for years, but with the flowering of San Francisco's hippy counterculture it was clear that the new music popularized by Elvis and then the Beatles was here to stay, and deepening and diversifying both creatively and in its audience. With a proven setting, improved concert P.A. equipment, and numerous rock/pop/folk acts seeking a showcase to bring them to national and—with the event to be filmed for a concert movie—international attention, the whole event was put together very quickly.

With the Beatles busy promoting their new masterpiece, *Sgt. Pepper's Lonely Hearts Club Band*, and in any case retired from the stage, they could not make it, while with their drugs possession trial imminent, neither could Mick and Keith of the Rolling Stones, though Brian Jones flew over as a VIP guest. That left as British representatives at the three-day event that the Who and—returning to his homeland as a UK rock sensation whose debut album, *Are You Experienced?*, had been kept off the top of the chart only by *Sgt. Pepper*—Jimi Hendrix, with his English backing musicians the Experience.

The rivalry came to a head when both bands were billed to play on Sunday night, June 18. Each band knew the other would put on a show calculated to make whoever followed sound like an anticlimax. They flipped for it, and the Who won.

Though Roger later boasted that his wizardly cape was in fact a tablecloth he'd bought in Shepherd's Bush market, the psychedelically dandified Who pulled out all the stops with their three latest singles and the mini-opera "A Quick One" before ending with the grand finale of "My

Generation" and smashing all their gear as smoke bombs clouded the stage.

The audience was stunned.

There was only one problem. Broke as ever, the Who's management had decided against airfreighting over the band's massive amplification system, so they made do with underpowered rented Vox amps. That became apparent when Jimi Hendrix took the stage, having brought his own gear with him. Serene in the decibels, he played a superb short set that culminated in the sacrifice of his guitar, set alight with lighter fluid—a stunt he'd invented three months

JUNE 16·17·18·1967

ABOVE: John marries sweetheart Alison Wise in London on June 23, 1967.

OPPOSITE: Poster for California's Monterey Pop Festival where the Who did battle with Jimi Hendrix on Sunday, June 18, 1967.

before in London—and then smashed.

Once again, Hendrix had upstaged the Who but not overshadowed them. Both acts had been sensational, but in the United States, Jimi's star would rise faster than that of his Track Records stablemates.

Splash! Bang!

Flying back to the UK, Keith planned to while away the time by dropping a new kind of super-strength hallucinogenic called STP supplied by the notorious San Francisco figure Owsley Stanley, the first private manufacturer of LSD. Thinking to

keep him company, the acid-hardened Pete realized he'd bitten off more than he could chew when he suffered a terrifying out-of-body experience beyond even his worst acid trip. Not only did he never touch STP again, but so disgusted was he that he even stopped smoking for four years. But he needed something to fill the visionary gap. It would come along soon enough.

Meanwhile, John had barely left the United States on honeymoon before he returned, on the Queen Elizabeth ocean liner, to New York with his long-standing sweetheart, Alison. While he was away, the three members left behind quickly recorded two

Stones songs in the event that Mick and Keith would be out of circulation in prison for a long time, having been found guilty of drug offenses. "The Last Time" and "Under My Thumb" were respectful but unexciting covers, and sold only moderately as the Who's rush-released new single. Mick and Keith, meanwhile, appealed their sentences, which were effectively rescinded when even the *Times* newspaper complained of injustice and persecution.

The Who were reunited back in the United States on their first full-blown tour, supporting English teen-pop sensations Herman's Hermits—as ludicrous a mismatch as Jimi Hendrix touring with the Monkees at the same time. Though they were performing to the wrong kind of audience, the Who were only having to play half-hour sets and so feeling relatively unpressurized. They bonded on the tour plane and in hotels as never before, and got along well, too, with the headliners. The partying was intense, famously getting most out of hand on Keith's birthday, August 23, at the Holiday Inn in Flint, Michigan, where they were all staying safely out of range of riot-torn Detroit. So they made their own riot. Nobody disputes the food fight, the defenestrated TVs, the sheriff, the arrests, the smashed teeth, and emergency dentists. But did Keith really drive a new Lincoln Continental parked outside into the hotel pool? Memories are fogged by drink and drugs, but the soberest member of the party, Roger, recalls that it really did happen. As for the singer—a bachelor again in all but legal status—he cut a swathe through America's girlhood to offset the pain of a tour that, thanks to his colleagues' destructiveness on and offstage, lost money, raising rather than reducing their mountain of debt.

ABOVE: The Who's rush-released cover version of two Rolling Stones songs to protest the jail sentences passed on Keith Richards and Mick Jagger in 1967.

RIGHT: The band pose with Roger's new Volvo P1800 in 1966.

The Who's notoriety, however, was climbing, thanks not least to their US network debut as guests on *The Smothers Brothers Comedy Hour* that September. Introduced by Tommy Smothers, who'd been wowed in the crowd at Monterey, the Who played a new song, "I Can See for Miles," and then, as was now traditional at the end of "My Generation," went into auto-destruct mode. Dissatisfied by the feeble combustion of his flash powder at dress rehearsal, for the performance itself Keith loaded the special effects cannon by his drums with a quantity well above safety level, its massive detonation shaking the TV cameras, filling the studio with smoke, injuring Keith's leg, singeing Pete's hair, and, he would later claim, permanently affecting his hearing in one ear. It was with some aplomb that he carried on with the show, smashing the guitar strapped around a stunned Smothers Brother's neck. Rumor has it that so shocked was a fellow guest, the movie legend Bette Davis, who was waiting in the wings to go on, that she fainted into the arms of Mickey Rooney.

On the tour, Pete listened obsessively to the Beatles' *Sgt. Pepper* and the Beach Boys' *Pet Sounds*. His ambitions above all being artistic, he pledged to himself that there was no point in carrying on in rock music unless he and the band could make a similar masterpiece. And in the songs they had been recording between shows in the UK and the United States, Pete was convinced they were on their way to doing just that. But would the public agree?

LEFT: Pete and Roger, rock's perennial odd couple.

chapter 9

Gambling on Genius

OF ALL THE YEARS in the six decades since the Elvis explosion gave shape and momentum to youth culture that resonates to this day, the strangest yet most pregnant with possibility was 1967.

For Pete, it was the year he maxed out the drugs and, after a flirtation with UFOs and ley lines, found a guru to fill the hole: Meher Baba. Nearing the end of his life and having long taken a vow of silence, the Indian spiritual master advocated, in Pete's words, "practical spirituality—do your best, don't worry, be happy." The idea of charity, working to help the neediest, and imagination being the means by which one realizes one's inner divinity were teachings that chimed with Pete, and whereas most pop stars had grown out of the their gurus by the '70s, he has followed Baba's teachings ever since.

LEFT: The Who touch down in Germany, 1967.

ABOVE: A smashing time at Granby Halls, Leicester, England, on March 13, 1967.
LEFT: The 1967 single "I Can See for Miles."

A month or two late, then, Pete got into the spirit of 1967's Summer of Love. Making a *Sgt. Pepper*–sized splash to launch the Who into the album era proved tougher. Over months, the Who had recorded a number of new songs, many showing the influence of the Beach Boys' *Pet Sounds* on sumptuously tender melodies and lush vocal harmonies, though his vignettes of love and longing tended to the bizarre—its tune almost Purcell-like, "Tattoo" followed "I'm a Boy" and "Pictures of Lily" in linking family life and gender insecurity or sexual shame. Pete had also had one of his visionary futuristic ideas such as that which proved the springboard for "I'm a Boy": again set in 1999, "Rael" was another fragmentary mini-opera based on the notion of Red China invading Israel. Album-opener "Armenia City in the Sky" was written by a musician friend from Ealing, John "Speedy" Keen, and showcased Pete's spectacular, effects-loaded psychedelic rock guitar.

Then there was the song Pete believed was his ace in the hole, written in 1966 but kept back for the moment when he felt the group needed a No. 1 single. Having spent all summer away from the UK—during which time acts in the Who vein, such as fellow former faux-mods the Small Faces and Birmingham's brilliant, stunt-driven band the Move, had moved in on their turf—he felt that time had come. "I Can See for Miles" was an intense, even obsessive rocker of high drama, and never had the band worked so hard on a recording.

Obsessed by the idea of a huge hit single even as he was trying to make an artistic statement album, Pete had a brainwave. Immersed that summer in American AM Top 40 radio, with its singles and jingles, Pete came home to find that its nearest UK equivalent—the commercial "pirate" stations moored offshore and beaming to the mainland, which had really been behind the Who since the start—had been outlawed. The BBC had taken some of these stations' now unemployed DJs to launch a national pop station, Radio 1, whose first record played was the Move's "Flowers in the Rain." Much as *Sgt. Pepper* used the linking device of the Beatles' alter-egos as a Victorian brass band, what would give the Who's new

THE WHO SELL OUT

Replacing the stale smell of excess with the sweet smell of success, Peter Townshend, who, like nine out of ten stars, needs it. Face the music with Odorono, the all-day deodorant that turns perspiration into inspiration.

THE WHO SELL OUT

This way to a cowboy's breakfast. Daltrey rides again. Thinks: "Thanks to Heinz Baked Beans every day is a super day". Those who know how many beans make five get Heinz beans inside and outside at every opportunity. Get saucy.

TOP RIGHT: David Montgomery took the photos that illustrate the album's running theme of commercialism.

RIGHT: *The Who Sell Out* album sleeve.

album its unity would be the concept of a commercial radio show, complete with jingles and even songs selling products. The sleeve would reflect that, too, with each of the four members selling a brand: Pete's would be Odorono deodorant, Keith's Medac acne cream, John's a Charles Atlas body-building course, and Roger's Heinz Baked Beans, with the singer photographed in a tub of the nutritious tinned legume.

Titled *The Who Sell Out*, the album followed the pattern of its two predecessors, with its December release coming in time for Christmas, but did less well, reaching only No. 13 in the UK but just scraping into the US Top 50. More worrying still, the single that heralded the album, "I Can See for Miles," failed to give the Who the UK No. 1 that Pete had banked on. It only just made No. 10. That it actually went one place higher in the United States, remaining the band's only Top 10 single in America, hardly alleviated Pete's bitter disappointment in his home nation's failing to recognize the work of which he was so proud.

Missing the Bus

What had gone wrong? Nothing, except the competition was stiffer for the Who now that they no longer had novelty on their side. The Beatles were bulletproof at No. 1 whatever happened, but even the Stones saw their stock dip in late '67 before turning things around with May '68's "Jumping Jack Flash."

ABOVE: Pete the artist and self-taught intellectual, at home.

For the Who, the silver lining came in the United States. Though *The Who Sell Out* didn't reach very high in the chart, it hung around for nearly six months. The Who were to undertake two long North American tours that year, their popularity growing as they adapted to the new rock show format of longer sets and older, more knowledgeable audiences than the hit-driven teeny-bop crowd that overtook the mods back in Britain in 1966 and '67.

Also taking off that year was FM radio, which tapped into the albums culture rather than Top 40 singles, and the burgeoning rock press, whose serious approach in interviews stimulated Pete to think out loud and develop new ideas on the hoof. Such was the growing power of their live musicianship that summertime's second tour was extended from three to nine weeks, and the Who would command the fourth-largest live fee on the circuit after the Jimi Hendrix Experience, Cream, and the Doors.

During a show that August with the Doors, a female fan who rushed the stage in worship of Jim Morrison's serpentine charisma fell and was badly injured, inspiring the song "Sally Simpson," one of several diverse elements that Pete was weaving into the work whose ambitious scope he believed was essential to sustaining and growing their US success and restoring their UK credibility as creative artists rather than no-longer-novel gimmicky sensationalists.

A full-length rock opera.

Where in the past Roger in particular might have bridled at such an idea, by 1968 he was renovating a picturesque medieval country-cottage home, and now had a comfortable lifestyle to maintain, complete with new girlfriend Heather Taylor, though there were still numerous dalliances on the road. He knew—as did John and Keith, both married men though at the opposite end of the spectrum of domestication—that the Who had either to step up boldly or be doomed to slide. Pete, too, had married that spring, to Karen Astley.

ABOVE: Keith, his wife, Kim, and daughter, Mandy: not a happy family.

BELOW: Pete marries Karen Astley on May 20, 1968.

For a while, the Who would be at peace among themselves, channeling their aggressive energy into a formidably exciting live act. Their last really bad behavior of the '60s—hotel trashing—came on tour in Australia and New Zealand, where the former country's officialdom gave them and their touring mates, the Small Faces, a very hard time. The Small Faces also targeted the mod crowd, and hailed mostly from east London, whereas the Who were from the west of the city. The two groups had a good rapport and mutual respect, and their paths would cross in the future, both personally and professionally. Soulfully cockney, the Small Faces rivaled the Who in the UK singles chart, and their April '68 hit "Lazy Sunday" cued up Pete's response in a similar vein: "Dogs," a pub-sing-along-style tribute to the dog track.

Amusing and zany but melodically unfocused, "Dogs" only made it to No. 25 in June, a flop that began to depress the band's appeal and live fee in the UK, so confirming their growing conviction that nothing less than a huge artistic statement

could reverse a perceptible and worrying homeland slide. Nor was this flop a blip. Road-tested live for months, the Bo Diddley–style R&B throwback "Magic Bus" had the irresistible simplicity and drive that "Dogs" lacked yet did no better when released in the UK in September.

TOP and ABOVE: 1968 was a bad year for hits, with flop singles and the misleadingly titled US-released album, a ragbag rather than live document of the Who on tour.

The Beatle, the Stones, and the Who

The opera that Pete was conceiving blended several preoccupations—the traumatic effect of war on parents and children, child abuse and bullying, the senses and sensory deprivation, bogus healers, LSD, the British holiday camp—into a tale of a young man's spiritual journey to adulation and back. While Kit encouraged Pete's thematic and formal ambitions, the songwriter drew also from long and helpful discussions on the road with the band, who were as eager as he was that this project should work. Songs were recorded and re-recorded as the band felt their way into this unknown territory of a long-form album where each song needed to have a standalone power as well as integrate into a narratively and thematically coherent whole.

An additional discipline was that the album had to be performable all the way through on the road, to utterly refresh the Who's box office appeal with a sense of real event. Yet the limitations of London's IBC studio determined that the music had a lightness and transparency very unlike their increasingly heavy, thunderous stage sound. It was an inconsistency the band could live with, as they could many others during the making of this album, which was as eclectic as it was overarching. The final piece of the jigsaw—the single that would herald and promote the album on daytime radio—came when Pete's friend, the young music critic Nik Cohn, promised the eventual album a rave review in the *New York Times* if he worked into it his current craze: pinball.

BELOW: The Who in 1967: the summer of love was never quite their season.

As Pete plotted the opera—variously given the working titles *Deaf, Dumb and Blind Boy*, *Amazing Journey*, *Journey into Space*, *The Brain Opera*, and *Omnibus* before Townshend settled on the everyman name of *Tommy*—and the material piled up, the recording sessions in London from that September lasted several weeks, with interruptions as the band played gigs to pay the hefty studio bills. (Track Records was short of cash by now, despite several hit albums and singles, including the worldwide smash "Fire!" by Pete's discovery, the Crazy World of Arthur Brown, principally because the huge Hendrix earners were subject to a rival recording contract claim.)

Of those end-of-'68 shows, one in particular from December stands out, though it was suppressed at the time. Wishing to live the hippie dream, several acts that year had ideas to take their shows to the people by rail, by horse-drawn caravan, or under the big top. Thwarted by the logistical nightmare of their bolder ideas, the Rolling Stones settled on a TV special to be called *The Rolling Stones Rock and Roll Circus*, featuring the band performing under canvas with a ringmaster, circus acts, an audience, and guest performers including John Lennon, Yoko Ono, Eric Clapton, Marianne Faithfull, Taj Mahal,

RIGHT: John and Keith mingle at *The Rolling Stones Rock and Roll Circus*, including (standing, from left) Stones' Bill Wyman, Charlie Watts, and Brian Jones, and (seated) Yoko Ono, Julian Lennon, John Lennon, and Eric Clapton.

Jethro Tull, and the Who. Production problems delayed the Stones' own performance, which, despite Mick Jagger's compelling presence, was tired, as was the audience. The Who on the other hand were fresh and fired up from the mini-opera "A Quick One, While He's Away," a highlight of the film. The film failed to showcase the Stones at their best, though, so they shelved the project, which remained unseen for years.

At last, by March 1969, *Tommy* was finished, with its first single, "Pinball Wizard," poised for release. For the Who, this two-disc rock opera, which had devoured so much time, money, and commitment, was their make-or-break album. But which way would it go?

ABOVE: John gearing up for the first US stop of the *Tommy* tour, at the Fillmore West, San Francisco.

LEFT: The single "Pinball Wizard."

OPPOSITE: The Who would steal the show at *The Rolling Stones Rock and Roll Circus*, a TV special that was shelved for decades.

chapter 10

The Big Stage

THE FIRST THE WORLD HEARD of *Tommy* was the urgently strummed sequence of B minor, B sus4, and B major chords on acoustic guitar that dramatically introduced the single, "Pinball Wizard," which was released on March 7, 1969, just as mixing was being completed on the album it heralded. The album's release would further lag behind that of the single, thanks to production delays on the sleeve, an intriguing and lavish foldout triptych produced by Mike McInnerney, the friend of Pete who had introduced him to the teachings of Meher Baba, who was also the art director of London's counterculture newspaper *IT* (*International Times*).

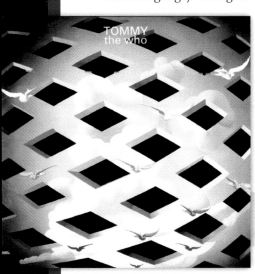

Encouragingly rising to No. 4, "Pinball Wizard" gave the Who their biggest UK hit in two years, stoking advance interest in the new album of a group who had seemed to be on the slide. Though the single was less successful in the United States, only just making the Top 20, the band believed that—once they performed the songs on the road—the album would sell, despite the Who's unhip record company Decca's feeble marketing efforts.

LEFT: The Who in 1969, on the brink of superstardom.

INSET: The album *Tommy*, its sleeve a rock-era classic.

The Who were right. After a set of shows and promotional media appearances in the UK just before the album's release, the band flew to America to play six weeks of gigs in such fan strongholds as New York and Detroit, and the album rose to No. 5, kept off the top by the original cast recording of the hippie Broadway musical *Hair*, the Fifth Dimension's pop-soul *Age of Aquarius*, the brass-rock of Blood Sweat & Tears' self-titled debut, and the soundtrack to Franco Zeffirelli's movie of *Romeo & Juliet*.

So far so good, but when the Who found live crowds responding with instant enthusiasm to the seventy-odd minutes dedicated to the opera, they knew that this was a show they could take on the road for months, if not years. And so they did, in effect rebooting the band they had been, from pop to rock, from mod to hippie, from ballroom to open-air festival. Gone was Roger's meticulous mod petal-cuts and bouffant styles; now his curls flew heroically free in time with the fringes of his shirts as he strutted bare-chested while Pete leaped and cartwheeled, visible to the back of the crowd in work boots and white boiler suit. Equally functional, Keith thrashed his drums in a T-shirt; in impassive contrast to them all, John thundered in fleet-fingered virtuosity, clad in a skeleton suit.

The hard roadwork of 1968 turned out to be crucial, not only for honing the band as a force to challenge the ring-rusty Rolling Stones when they eventually returned to the road in 1969 but also to hold their own against the UK's new rock sensations, Led Zeppelin, founded by Jimmy Page but named by John Entwistle and riding high with a hit debut album whose sleeve had been Keith Moon's idea. Pete in particular was finding himself in a stratospheric zone of performance onstage, which by now was highly athletic thanks to his powerful physique and a period of clean living.

"Welcome to this house,
Be one of us,
Come into this house.
Be one of us,
Come to our house,
Come to this house."

3/6

ABOVE: From *Tommy*, the single "See Me, Feel Me."

LEFT: The 1969 UK tour book.

RIGHT: In 1969, Roger emerged as the bare-chested rock god of the Age of Aquarius.

ABOVE: Fringe festival: Roger rocks Woodstock.

Like an animal protecting his territory, he had no truck with anyone taking what he saw as his stage, and got into trouble that May in New York when he booted a plainclothes policeman, there to evacuate the venue when the store next door was firebombed, from the stage. Three months later, Pete again repelled a stage invader, bashing him on the head with his Gibson SG guitar. This took place at the most famous rock gig of all time when, despite playing what they thought was a substandard show, the gods smiled on the Who. Their performance was one of the most triumphant and certainly spectacular one muddy August weekend in upstate New York, at the Woodstock Music & Art Fair (An Aquarian Exposition: 3 Days of Peace & Music). Or, as it's been universally known ever since, Woodstock.

Rocking the Woodstock Nation

Though preceded by Monterey and other rock festivals, by virtue of its huge crowds—some 400,000 people, many of them gatecrashers—stellar performers, and the hit movie and soundtrack album that captured the weekend and brought it to the masses in 1970, Woodstock was a milestone not only in the counterculture, where it has been immortalized as the ultimate tribal gathering, but also in the music industry, which now had an event to showcase just how much money there was to be made in the mud and in record stores afterward.

Woodstock was a happy collision of hippie idealism and the dollar bill, and the Who, for all Pete's spirituality, were strictly in it for the money. Dismayed at seeing a serious accident befall a tripping reveler, and less than amused by witnessing Keith and John—whose wife Alison was staying at a nearby motel with Pete's wife Karen and their baby daughter—being orally serviced by groupies, the guitarist was in no mood to align with the event's good vibrations. With *Tommy* flying off the shelves, the Who were one of the very biggest draws on the circuit and would not accept the promoters' check. Only cash would do and, with hard-nosed tour manager John "Wiggy" Wolff threatening a no-show unless the band got their money upfront, the local bank manager had to be helicoptered in—the roads being impassable, thanks to the crowds—to override the safe's time lock.

ABOVE: Downpours, mud, brown acid...but great music: the original Woodstock.

Going on six hours later than their scheduled 10:00 p.m. Saturday start, the Who were tired and irritated, and all but Roger were coming off LSD trips (Keith by choice and John and Pete having had their drinks spiked). But even at half power, their hour-long performance was electrifying and provided memorable moments, not only when Pete ejected hippie activist Abbie Hoffman from the stage, but also when the sun rose as the Who ended with their set with "My Generation," to which Pete added a coda of *Tommy* themes, new riffs, and sound effects as he hammered his guitar on the stage before hurling it, still live, into the pit.

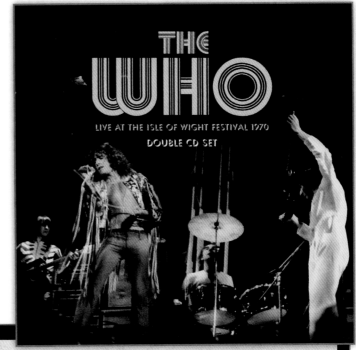

ABOVE: Released decades later on CD and DVD, The Who at 1970's Isle of Wight Festival captures their *Tommy*-era peak.

BELOW: In his white boiler suit, Pete resembled a spiritual mechanic on stage.

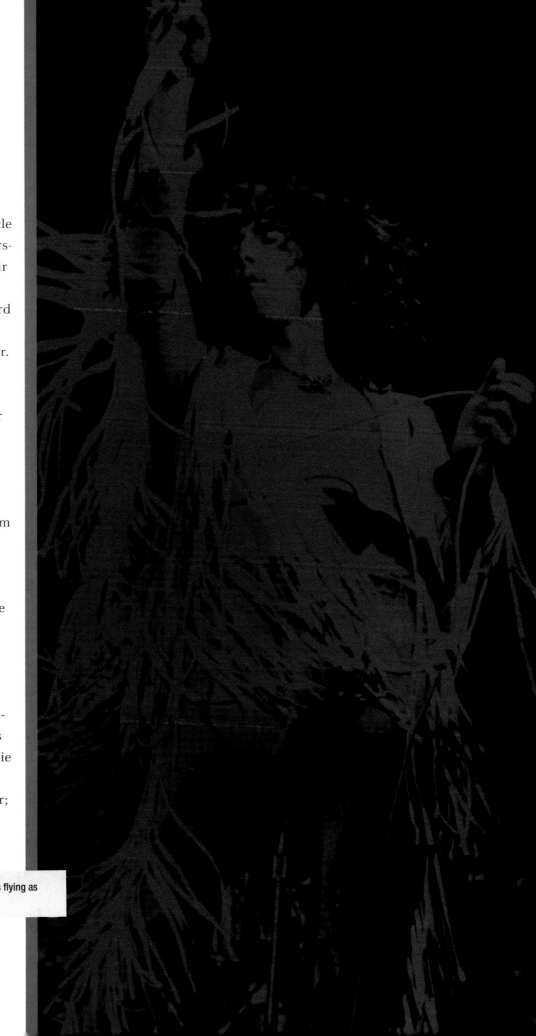

Two weeks later, on August 30, the Who were again helicoptered to a huge rock festival, back closer to home turf on the Isle of Wight, when Bob Dylan played his first full concert anywhere since his fabled turning-point motorcycle accident in 1966. Though Keith was nursing a fractured ankle, the Who met their best standard with machinelike precision, not even hanging around afterward to see the headliner who had been such an inspiration to Pete a few years earlier.

That year's Isle of Wight festival attracted 150,000 fans; exactly a year later, more than four times that number packed on to the island to see the Who again on a bill where the special attraction was Jimi Hendrix, who would be dead less than three weeks later.

These festival shows preserve on film and in pictures the most iconic phase of the Who's career: Roger the rock god, golden curls and fringed sleeves flying as he lariats his microphone; Pete the proletarian art thug thrashing and windmilling his cherry-red Gibson SG, with photographs freeze-framing him mid-leap; John jokily saturnine in his skeleton suit, singing the boss/congressman parts from the bottom of his boots in the Who's incendiary version of Eddie Cochran's "Summertime Blues" while his fingers effortlessly roll bass thunder; Keith, a gurning, twirling blur of arms, sticks, and impishness.

RIGHT: Roger the rock god, golden curls and fringed sleeves flying as he lariats his microphone.

Bottle the Lightning

Back before videos, DVDs, and the Internet, only if you checked out the *Woodstock* movie or the band's very rare TV appearances would you be able to get close to experiencing the full visual assault short of seeing an actual Who show—and at these mega-festivals, before jumbo screens came in, they might only be dots in the distance. Which is where the live album came in. You could not easily see the show, but especially following Woodstock's showcasing of the immersive live rock experience, you could certainly hear it. To beat the boom in pirated "bootleg" live albums, the years 1969–1971 saw an explosion of official rock live albums to souvenir and sell the stage show. By common acclaim, the Who's *Live at Leeds* is not just the best of the era but perhaps the greatest live rock album of all time.

From the very start, *Tommy* had been planned as a piece of music that could, with a few cuts, be played live as the heart of a new Who show, and so it proved, occupying well over an hour of a set that now routinely overran by two hours. Proud of how well they were performing this new set, the Who were routinely recording their American shows with a view to picking the best performances for release. Come New Year 1970, they were faced with eighty hours of tapes to review; unable to face it, Pete ordered engineer Bob Pridden to burn the lot. Instead, the band would set up two dates from which to pick the best for a live album. Though some material escaped the conflagration, Pridden obeyed his boss, who later regretted the fact that

ABOVE: The Who headline 1970's Isle of Wight Festival in front of as many as 600,000 fans, mostly gatecrashers.

OPPOSITE: Pete the proletarian art thug thrashing and windmilling his cherry-red Gibson SG.

he had been taken so literally; like a British summer's day, Pete was notoriously moody, and when storm clouds blotted out his sunny side, people knew better than to argue.

On February 14 and 15, the Who played and recorded shows at universities in Leeds and nearby Hull in the unromantic industrial north of England, and on both nights they were captured in terrific form. The acoustics of the two halls were very different, Hull being much more echo-y, with the recording also failing to pick up John's bass in the early numbers. So Leeds it was perforce, the two-hour show cherry-picked to give forty minutes of blistering rock, including covers of "Summertime Blues" and other old favorites, Mose Allison's "Young Man Blues" and Johnny Kidd & the Pirates' "Shakin' All Over," plus the singles "I Can't Explain" and "Substitute," and, taking up a whole side, augmented versions of "Magic Bus" and "My Generation."

Packaged like a bootleg for release that May, the album reproduced memorabilia of the band they so recently had been—indebted, mod, and mad—alongside a new picture of Pete leaping against the Woodstock sunrise, symbolizing the band they now were. It was the '70s now, and in the new era of larger-than-life, louder-than-life superhero rock, the Who were among the biggest and baddest on the block.

ABOVE: The iconic faux-bootleg *Live at Leeds* album.

LEFT: The Who in 1967; two years later, they really did have lift-off.

chapter 11

Teenage Wasteland

WITH THE MONEY rolling in from both *Tommy* and live performances, the Who were out of debt and no longer under pressure to make it big or break up.

They were now under a new kind of pressure: to follow up their own blockbuster. Some of this pressure was external; many new fans were confused, thinking that the band was called Tommy and their album called *The Who*. This grew less amusing as 1970 wore on, and they realized that *Tommy* could become a straitjacket, restricting the band by closing fans' minds to anything new and different. But mostly the pressure came from within: from Pete's artistic ambition to create work of total emotional and spiritual engagement, using every medium and technique at his command. This included film, in which he was intensely interested, and encouraged by experimental moviemaking friends. Throughout 1970, Pete in all good faith tried to get a collaborative enterprise off the ground that integrated film and music, but nothing clicked.

LEFT: The Who's sound grew heavier and more intense in the early '70s.

In the end, Pete was an auteur, a lone wolf—an artist adding to his techniques and skills base all the time to try to keep up with his growing, if nebulous, conceptual ambitions. Though he would later claim that Benjamin Britten's *Billy Budd* was his principal inspiration for *Tommy*, his wider artistic inspiration was Richard Wagner with his concept of "Gesamtkunstwerk," the all-embracing, multimedia art form most fully realized in the composer's *Ring Cycle* of operas—a boxed set of which sat in Pete's home studio. With Karen and a young, growing family to take care of, Pete now lived by the Thames in Twickenham, west London, where his home studio was now capable of creating demos, including drums and keyboards, to releasable standard.

Pete was also taking a keen and knowledgeable interest in synthesizers, much as the youth prodigy Stevie Wonder (a favorite Motown musician of his since the mid-'60s) was about to do on the other side of the Atlantic. Though synthesizers at that point were still mostly monophonic, Pete was experimenting with playing his polyphonic electric organ via an EMS VCS3 synth, modifying its sound, and getting to grips too with the gigantic ARP 2500

ABOVE: Pete in his Twickenham home studio in 1969…

RIGHT: …which, within a year, became packed with synthesizer equipment.

synth. Though both the Byrds and Beatles had dabbled with synths in the late '60s, the Who would be one of the very first rock bands to use the technology not just to texture but to structure their music.

Though an anti-Semite and in other respects a despicable man, Wagner had a higher purpose for his art: to attain for his audience a transcendent spiritual level. Pete shared that ambition. He felt that there were moments while the band performed *Tommy* live in 1969 and 1970 when the music connected so deeply with the audience that a sense of profound communion swept from fans to stage and back. "I've seen moments in Who gigs where the vibrations were becoming so pure that I thought the whole world was just going to stop, the whole thing was just becoming so unified," he said.

Tommy had spiritual themes and messages but was not designed to take the audience to the spiritual heights that Pete now believed was possible. His next major work would set its sights even higher. It would be a work with a concept, a plot, and numerous themes—but no end. Called *Lifehouse*, it started out as a number of songs he had written while still touring *Tommy* and reflecting that experience, coalesced into enough of an idea to be workshopped interactively with fans, hit a dead end, nearly cause the band to break up, rupture their rapport with Kit Lambert, and yet finally result in a huge hit album, a classic that remains many fans' favorite. Nor did the *Lifehouse* project end there; it has continued to morph and resurface in the career of Pete and the Who to the present day, forty-five years after its inception.

TOP and ABOVE: Pete and Roger at full throttle in October 1970.

OPPOSITE: The Who perform on BBC TV's *Into '71* on December 30, 1970, with Pete as Pearly King and Roger in heels.

The Seeker and the Search

Where *Tommy* drew in a number of different elements to create its patchwork whole, *Lifehouse* arose from Pete's belief that a number of ideas he was toying with could be united into a coherent whole. Among them was the idea of the conflicted seeker after truth—exemplified in "The Seeker," the Who's only release of new material, as a single, between *Tommy* in 1969, and the *Lifehouse* distillation/spinoff album, *Who's Next*, in 1971. Ever mindful that Roger sang his songs while not necessarily sharing all his values and views, Pete wrote a sprightly, witty rock song about a spiritual seeker with a rough, tough streak who has looked to Bob Dylan and the Beatles for the answer to the unspecified big questions but not found the answer, and does not expect to "until the day I die."

"The Seeker" was a minor hit in spring 1970; that it did not sell better was no longer the problem it would have been two years earlier, with the Who now firmly established as an albums band in an era when the likes of Pink Floyd could barely be bothered to release singles and Led Zeppelin positively refused to, lest it cheapen their mystique.

TOP: The single "The Seeker."

ABOVE: Recording "The Seeker" with manager and producer Kit Lambert in London's IBC Studios on January 19, 1970.

OPPOSITE: At the housewarming party and press launch for *Who's Next* at Keith's new home in Chertsey, south of London, on July 14, 1971.

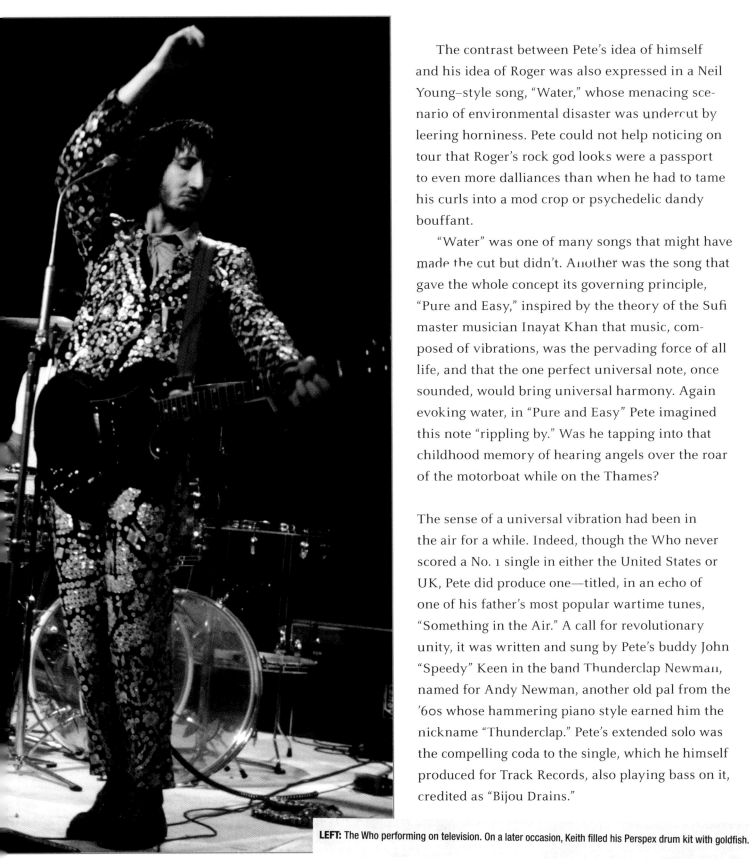

The contrast between Pete's idea of himself and his idea of Roger was also expressed in a Neil Young–style song, "Water," whose menacing scenario of environmental disaster was undercut by leering horniness. Pete could not help noticing on tour that Roger's rock god looks were a passport to even more dalliances than when he had to tame his curls into a mod crop or psychedelic dandy bouffant.

"Water" was one of many songs that might have made the cut but didn't. Another was the song that gave the whole concept its governing principle, "Pure and Easy," inspired by the theory of the Sufi master musician Inayat Khan that music, composed of vibrations, was the pervading force of all life, and that the one perfect universal note, once sounded, would bring universal harmony. Again evoking water, in "Pure and Easy" Pete imagined this note "rippling by." Was he tapping into that childhood memory of hearing angels over the roar of the motorboat while on the Thames?

The sense of a universal vibration had been in the air for a while. Indeed, though the Who never scored a No. 1 single in either the United States or UK, Pete did produce one—titled, in an echo of one of his father's most popular wartime tunes, "Something in the Air." A call for revolutionary unity, it was written and sung by Pete's buddy John "Speedy" Keen in the band Thunderclap Newman, named for Andy Newman, another old pal from the '60s whose hammering piano style earned him the nickname "Thunderclap." Pete's extended solo was the compelling coda to the single, which he himself produced for Track Records, also playing bass on it, credited as "Bijou Drains."

LEFT: The Who performing on television. On a later occasion, Keith filled his Perspex drum kit with goldfish.

"We've got to get together sooner or later," goes one line; less than two years later, it would be echoed as "Let's get together before we get much older" by Pete in a key *Lifehouse* song written as its first number, and starting the story off with Ray, a Scottish farmer in the dystopian future—"a teenage wasteland." With his wife Sally (presumably *Tommy*'s Sally Simpson, now grown up), Ray heads to the polluted south in search of his daughter, Mary, run away to attend a rock concert in defiance of the government who have confined people to virtual-reality Lifesuits plugged into the Grid mainframe that has been hacked by the hero of the story, Bobby, whose name was the original working title of the work, and the successor to Tommy. Each member of the concert audience has been data-mined for personality, star-sign, and so on, this information converted into individualized songs. Just as the police storm the Lifehouse, each song converges in a pure, perfect note whose vibration dematerializes the audience into a rapture-like nirvana.

Though Pete's 1970 vision—which gained shape and detail over months in several self-exploratory media interviews—might strike some as farfetched

ABOVE: Skilled musicians John and Pete at the keyboard in 1970.

RIGHT: A transcendent stage moment, inspiring the *Lifehouse* project.

INSET: The number one hit single "Something in the Air" produced by Pete in 1969 for his friends, the band Thunderclap Newman.

even by the standards of fantasy fiction, his predictions of the Internet, virtual reality, and environmental degradation were uncanny. Not for the last time would he see deeply where we're heading.

What Was He Going on About?

Pete pictured the project reaching the public not only as another double album like *Tommy* but as a movie and an interactive concert. Vital to proceedings was quadrophonic sound, as pioneered by Pete's friends in Pink Floyd. With Pete's expansive

concepts proving a struggle, though, movie interest cooled. But, as in the *Lifehouse* concert, Pete was determined to go for a new kind of Who concert experience with a storyline and characters based on workshopping, and astrological and personality profile input from audience members. Having seen a performance of Samuel Beckett's *Waiting for Godot* at London's Young Vic Theatre the previous summer, Pete felt this was the ideal space, and in January and February 1971 he and the band tried to make it work over several consecutive Mondays.

There was one huge problem, however: no one really grasped what Pete wanted to happen or was even going on about. And that included not only the audience that had wandered in off the street but the band itself. They did though certainly understand that Pete needed to give himself a huge artistic challenge that would speak to his spiritual preoccupations as well as his creative ambition to stimulate the stream of great songs the Who needed to move on from *Tommy* and sustain their career. Taking the lead, the ever-practical Roger tried his best to reconnect Pete to what could be re-alistically achieved. John, meanwhile, had his own debut solo album to mix, a process that took longer than its actual recording but would result that May in the macabre and blackly humorous hard-rock set *Smash Your Head against the Wall*.

Keith, meanwhile, now had good reason to seek oblivion. The year previously, on January 4, 1970, while outside a pub he was fleeing after being attacked by skinheads, he drunkenly drove his Bentley into his friend, driver, and bodyguard Neil Boland, killing him. Though it was an acci-dent, Keith was haunted ever afterward. Rather than sobering him up, though, the tragedy only intensified his looning, in which he had willing cronies in the comically inspired Vivian Stanshall and "Legs" Larry Smith of the Bonzo Dog Band, pals of his from the after-hours club circuit. Their pranking included dressing as vicars, gorillas, and, least amusingly, Hitler and Himmler in London's Jewish neighborhood of Golders Green, where they were chased down the street by a cleaver-wielding storekeeper. As Pete's fruit-less experiment at the Young Vic dragged on, Keith alleviated his frustration and boredom with a stream of groupies forming a line at his Winnebago.

Finally admitting defeat, Pete agreed to a plan to regroup and record some of the new songs in New York, where he hoped to find support from his mentor Kit. A year earlier, thanks to a broken jaw, Kit had to leave the production of "The Seeker" to Pete, and now the guitarist found his co-manager and mentor in the grip of heroin addiction and no longer seeing eye-to-eye. Back when the Who were touring *Tommy*, Kit had scored a tremendous coup by booking them to perform in some of the world's great opera houses, conferring official prestige on his protégés' meisterwerk. Though pleased to be applauded by the likes of Leonard Bernstein, the Who felt disconnected from the energy of the rock crowd and came to feel they were fulfilling Kit's fantasy rather than their own, especially when Kit

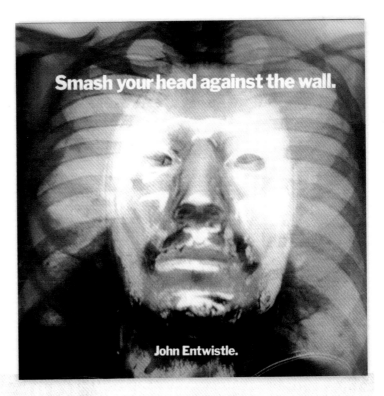

ABOVE: John's debut solo album, *Smash Your Head against the Wall*, released in May 1971.

OPPOSITE: Traumatized and guilt-ridden after accidentally killing his chauffeur Neil Boland on January 4, 1970, Keith grew ever more manic.

seemed to want to keep *Tommy* going, promoting stage and movie productions long after the band had grown tired of it and wanted to move on. Pete then overheard Kit disparaging him to Anya Butler, while Kit's antics in the recording studio were beginning to prove obstructive and annoying rather than cheerfully stimulating. The bond between the Who's creative force and the man who had done so much to nurture their creativity and artistic ambition started to fray.

Meet the New Boss

Following his curious recruitment of Mountain's Leslie West to play lead guitar, Pete's hopes for the New York sessions foundered, and the band returned to the UK, reuniting with Shel Talmy's old engineer Glyn Johns, who in the intervening five years had built a formidable reputation with the Beatles, the Rolling Stones, Led Zeppelin, and Traffic as the best rock engineer in the business. At first brought in to record a number of shows where the Who would road-test new songs—most written for or shoehorned into Pete's *Lifehouse* concept— Glyn would eventually get to the point he had wanted all along: to produce the best of these songs for a regular rock album.

Pete was not the only one interested in movies and a bolder, more encompassing way of presenting the band than the conventional album-tour-album cycle, so months of ever-changing plans and loose ends followed before the Who found themselves doing exactly the conventional thing they had wanted to avoid. Yet they did it with magnificent results.

To get to the point of abandoning the grand idea of *Lifehouse*, Pete exhausted everyone he trusted in the search for someone who understood, but to no avail. He had, he admits, a nervous breakdown of sorts—and, backsliding from a relatively clean-living period during the late '60s, was now hitting the brandy bottle. But with the band trusting in Glyn Johns' know-how and wild enthusiasm for the best of the songs Pete had written, if not the framework that had stimulated them, that summer the Who reconvened in west London's Olympic Studios, reuniting too with pianist Nicky Hopkins, and cut what many maintain is the album of their career—and one of the very best by any rock band.

Lifehouse's "teenage wasteland" opener was tightened up to create one of the most dramatic of all opening tracks, its modulating, cyclical keyboard loop inspired by composer Terry Riley, in particular his works *In C* and *A Rainbow in Curved Air*, while its instrumental outro, played by violinist Dave Arbus of the group East of Eden, was Indian in flavor, in a nod to Meher Baba, the two elements combining in the song's title, "Baba O'Riley." In between, Roger never sounded more heroic, the band more dramatic.

As the album, offhandedly titled *Who's Next*, unspooled to fans upon its release that August of 1971, its moods and flavors changed before closing with a barnstormer even more epic than the opener, which also rode a synthesized keyboard loop.

RIGHT: Pete in full flight.

OPPOSITE: Pete and Keith get animated at the press launch for *Who's Next* at Keith's new home, a futuristic bungalow called Tara House.

Inspired in part by hippie squatters living near Pete, "Won't Get Fooled Again" provided his most quoted lyric since "My Generation" six years before: "Here comes the new boss—same as the old boss." Its witty rebuttal of revolutionary or leadership change was packaged in a blisteringly high-energy rock anthem, edited down from its album-length eight minutes to three for single release to herald the album. *Who's Next* was a big hit in the United States, the UK, and elsewhere despite—or perhaps assisted by—a sleeve depicting the four band members having just relieved themselves against a concrete obelisk mysteriously sat in the middle of a slagheap.

Despite falling far short of Pete's original ambitions, *Who's Next* was almost the ideal follow-up to *Tommy*, being hugely popular yet very different, its sound, apart from anything else, engineered for maximum wallop as well as finesse by Glyn Johns. A fund of great songs from which the band could pick and choose in their live sets, rather than have to present them in sequence, it gave the

group enormous new flexibility as they hit the road again, with record crowds and ticket sales including thirty-five thousand at London's Oval Cricket Ground in a benefit show for relief of refugees in Bangladesh. Further proof of the Who's popularity came that fall with the release of the singles collection *Meaty, Beaty, Big, and Bouncy*, a Top 10 album on both sides of the Atlantic.

With *Lifehouse*, Pete had lost the plot but got his mojo working even better than before. Though it had worn him down to the breaking point, convinced nobody, driven the rest of the Who to distraction, and strained his bond with Kit Lambert, *Lifehouse* was an idea he could not let go. Not released on *Who's Next*, other songs like the 1971 UK single "Let's See Action," and, a few years later, the theme-crystallizing "Pure and Easy," would surface. And Pete would revisit the concept, adding songs and morphing the storyline but keeping the same themes. Whatever he had learned from the huge success of compromising his great schemes for the sake of band harmony and getting something actually done, Pete refused to change one thing:

Whatever happened, he would continue to think big.

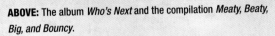

ABOVE: The album *Who's Next* and the compilation *Meaty, Beaty, Big, and Bouncy.*

RIGHT: The singles "Won't Get Fooled Again" and "Let's See Action."

OPPOSITE: September 18, 1971, headlining at the Oval Cricket Ground in South London.

chapter 12

Quad!

THE *LIFEHOUSE* EXPERIENCE had taken the Who to breaking point, five years after their previous near miss. Only the realization—once Glyn Johns entered the scene to offer some perspective and fresh enthusiasm—that Pete's songs were far too good not to properly record and take on tour refocused their united sense of purpose.

But months of bafflement and delay had taken their toll, and once the band came off the road from the second highly lucrative and wildly well-received US tour of 1971, they paused to recharge their batteries. Roger had bought a large house in Sussex, which, ever practical and hands-on, he then started to work on. Keith had a new house, too: Tara, a futuristic pile in Surrey where he hosted insane parties, when not looning in attendance of whatever fresh distraction caught his fancy, which for a while meant the parody doo-wop group Sha Na Na. Though not a huge seller, John's solo debut pleased its perfectionist maker, and, also enjoying new fatherhood, he set to work on a successor, released in November 1972 as *Whistle Rymes*.

Pete, meanwhile, in response to the bootlegging of two albums he made for private circulation to fellow followers of Meher Baba, collected a number of devotional songs, home studio demos, and unreleased songs he deemed unsuited to the Who in his first commercially released solo album, *Who Came First*. Though naughtily trading on the word "Who" in its title and the cover image of Pete in trademark stage bovver boots and boiler suit, its introspective, uncrunching nature restricted its sale to Who completists.

LEFT and INSET: John and his second solo album, *Whistle Rymes*.

RIGHT: Pete's first commercially released solo album, *Who Came First*.

FAR RIGHT: Pete in his studio with a photo of his guru, Meher Baba, in the background.

BELOW RIGHT: "Join Together" and "Relay," the Who's successful and not-so-successful, respectively, singles.

Though *Lifehouse* had been officially abandoned as a group project, especially since its partial release as *Who's Next*, Pete's train of creative thought could not be so easily derailed. That project's themes of transcendent communion between musicians and audience were the basis of the standalone Who single "Join Together," a cheerful sing-along groove with the unique hook of its signature sound being twanged on the busker's instrument called a Jew's harp. A Top 10 hit in the UK in June 1972 and Top 20 in the United States the following month, it kept the Who in the public consciousness during some low-profile months. Less successful was its successor, released at the end of the year. "Relay" had all the Who's guitar crunch and lurched along on almost funky rhythm, but its lyric, which called for unity in the teeth of surveillance, was as vague as its melody, and the singles buyer was not impressed.

These songs—*Lifehouse* afterthoughts—were also mooted for a soon-abandoned concept album provisionally titled *Rock Is Dead—Long Live Rock!*, which was Pete's admittedly self-conscious meditation on the Who, their fans, and the concept of a transcendent state of spiritual being attainable at peak musical moments. That May and June of 1972, the Who reconvened with Glyn Johns to record songs for this project, but on this occasion

the sessions were suspended by Pete because he felt that he had an even better idea, into which he wished to fit two of the songs they'd started, "Is It in My Head?" and "Love, Reign O'er Me."

It had been eight years since Keith had joined the band, as the final piece in the jigsaw, which meant they had now lasted longer than the Beatles had after their drummer, Ringo, joined the group. To Pete, this longevity as a four-piece of wildly contrasting individuals called for reflection—and a creative transformation into another rock opera, a form that offered the kind of scope and challenge that he felt most stimulated him. He had already toyed with quadraphonic sound live and in the studio, and the coincidence of there being four outputs in quadraphonic sound as there were four members of the Who created a connection that developed into the concept of a single character combined from the four members of the Who. Following *Tommy*'s Tommy and *Lifehouse*'s Bobby,

ABOVE and BELOW LEFT: The Who rock Paris as 400,000 attend a benefit gig for the French Communist Party, September 1972.

BELOW: Keith with "Legs" Larry Smith at the Crystal Palace Bowl in London, June 3, 1972.

this new character would be called Jimmy—and, as the subsequent liner notes put it, in describing the four-way split of his personality, "Schizophrenic? I'm bleeding Quadrophrenic." Combining the "tough guy" (Roger), the "romantic" (John), the "bloody lunatic" (Keith), and the "beggar, a hypocrite" (a self-flagellating Pete), Jimmy looked less quadrophrenic than just the kind of confused adolescent boy who had always sustained the Who's fan base, to which the Who were never more connected than in their mod days. So Jimmy would be a mod, his situation and storyline a composite of people the band knew, in particular Pete Meaden and their most devoted fan, "Irish" Jack Lyons.

Though the various elements of the opera album to be titled *Quadrophenia* did not click all in one go, and there were hiccups along the way, they fell into place with a speed that gave a structure for Pete to work on, and which the other three, on this occasion, had no trouble grasping. The concept was sound; it only needed to be executed, starting with Pete writing, arranging, and demoing more songs.

LEFT: Roger—"See Me, Feel Me..."

BELOW (from left): The Who's *Quadrophenia* album, the slipcase to Lou Reizner's *Tommy*, and the album within.

The Four on Detour

But there would be delays. Overshadowing the creative birth of the new rock opera, there came a stellar reboot of the old one. Music impresario Lou Reizner had produced Rod Stewart's first two solo albums, and the former "Rod the Mod" was by now one of the biggest rock stars in the world, both as a standalone performer and as front man for the Faces, the group that emerged from the ashes of the Who's old pals and fellow London faux-mod band the Small Faces. The previous year, *Tommy* had been adapted for ballet in Quebec and staged as an opera in Seattle, with Bette Midler in two roles, as financed by promoter Lou Adler, a leading figure behind the Monterey Pop festival five years before.

Reizner had more ambitious plans—a fully orchestrated new album with an all-star cast. Eight months in production with the London Symphony Orchestra and a sixty-voice choir, *Tommy* would have starred Rod in the title role until the Who decided to reclaim their own opera—and, so they hoped, lay it to rest. Rod was relegated to the role of the "Local Lad" who sang "Pinball Wizard" while Pete narrated, Roger reprised Tommy, and John performed as the bullying Cousin Kevin, while Keith was happy to leave his Uncle Ernie role to his pal Ringo, taking the role back in a concert performance the following March in Melbourne, Australia. Other star guests included Sandy Denny, Steve Winwood, Richie Havens, Graham Bell, Maggie Bell, and Merry Clayton. Released in October 1972, the album was an immediate best-seller, and was staged in a concert version that December at the Rainbow Theatre, London. For the first time, Pete could witness Roger singing live without being hyped up himself, and duly found a new respect for his bandmate's artistry as a vocal character actor.

ABOVE: Pete helps his friend Eric Clapton at the guitar legend's comeback concert at London's Rainbow Theatre on January 13, 1973.

In early 1973, Roger recorded a solo album, co-produced by singer-turned-actor (and later financial journalist) Adam Faith (né Terry Nelhams), a tough and enterprising working-class guy from Acton with whom Roger was always likely to hit it off. Produced at his home studio in Sussex, *Daltrey* showcased a softer, schmaltzier Roger than the public knew from the Who, selling respectably and spawning the UK Top 5 single "Giving It All Away," cowritten by Leo Sayer, whose own singer/songwriter career would soon take off.

That success worried Kit Lambert and Chris Stamp, lest it should tempt Roger away from the Who. In turn, Roger was growing suspicious about where the money was going. Meanwhile, John was using his Who downtime to work on his second and then third solo albums. And, aside from keeping the Who's name in the press thanks to his stream of stunts and pranks, Keith, who had played a tiny cameo in Frank Zappa's 1971 avant-garde movie *200 Motels*, now had a meatier part to play in *That'll Be the Day*, a movie which, like the *Quadrophenia* currently taking shape in Pete's head and home studio, looked back at rock's past. Stealing every scene in which he appeared as manic drummer J. D. Clover, Keith augmented a cast including teeny-bop star David Essex, '60s British pop star Billy Fury, and Keith's Beatles buddy Ringo Starr in a movie chronicling the rise of a scuffling musician in the UK's pre-Beatlemania rock scene.

All of this would, inadvertently, come to the aid of *Quadrophenia*. Rivaling the Stones and far more than Pink Floyd or Led Zeppelin, each member of the Who was impressing his own individual character on the public consciousness. By the time *Quadrophenia* came out, the four component parts of the composite Jimmy would be quite well known.

ABOVE: Keith and his daughter, Mandy, at home with his vehicle collection, including a hovercraft and trashed Ferrari Dino.

INSET: Roger's self-titled debut solo album.

The Knock-Out Punch

The major project that Pete was composing and the other members of the Who were raring to record would take time to come together in the studio. Never entirely happy in whichever commercial studio they had used before, they decided to invest in their own, tailored to their exact needs. They acquired an old church hall tucked away near the River Thames in Battersea, south London, but it took time to convert and install the recording console, mixing desk, and tape machines they wanted. It wasn't until May 1973 that Ramport Studios was ready to receive them, and even then to get the job done they needed to borrow the mobile studio equipment belonging to Pete's friend and fellow follower of Meher Baba, Ronnie Lane, the former Small Face and Face. With it came Ron Nevison, who ended up engineering *Quadrophenia*. Glyn Johns, meanwhile, was no longer on board; as with *Tommy*, Pete felt he needed the big-picture thinking of Kit Lambert to help him focus his ideas and fill in any gaps, despite their strained relationship over the previous eighteen months. Roger was skeptical; aside from feeling Kit and Chris were not backing his solo album, the audit he had commissioned on the Who's income revealed a worrying black hole where funds had mysteriously gone missing.

Kit had barely returned to recording with the Who when he was thrown out; half unhinged, he was of no use to Pete, who then moved to join Roger in taking legal action against their manager when he discovered a lot of his publishing money had gone missing, too. Promoted from within the backroom staff to take care of business, Bill Curbishley had proved himself shrewd and businesslike, and far more mindful than Kit, who had demons of his own, of the volatile chemistry within the group that would need careful handling. All his diplomatic skills would be needed in the years to come, starting that summer.

So detailed were the *Quadrophenia* demos that Pete brought in as guides to the rest of the band that building up each song often meant little more than filling in the gaps. His synthesizer was far too cumbersome to move from his home, so that is where he recorded the extensive synth parts; likewise, John's brass parts, of which there were over fifty on the finished album, were recorded at his home studio. Roger got in on the act too, working on his vocal parts in his Barn Studio so they would be perfect by the time he laid them down at Ramport. As for Keith, his crowning moment came in the opera's climax, "Love, Reign O'er Me," when, on July 17, the track was completed with a percussion freak-out.

Keith's pal Ringo was visiting the studio that day. "I always say that his timing was way off—he had no real sense of timing. That's how Keith played.

ABOVE: The single "5.15."
OPPOSITE: The band showing some camaraderie on stage, 1973.

Pete did all the parts on the original tracks and then got the band in to play them. I had a friend who wasn't in the music business and we went along to a Who recording session. They had a huge rack of tubular bells, and Keith ran at them from one end of the studio and dived into the bells, which they were recording. My friend said to me, 'Does everybody record like that?' I said no, hahahaha! You don't run into the instruments. Only Keith recorded like that, God bless him."

And then there was the rainstorm that flooded the isolation booth in the studio where pianist Chris Stainton of Joe Cocker's Grease Band—who had shared bills with the Who in 1968 and '69—was laying down his part for, of all songs, "Drowned." It was a rare drama in a surprisingly serene recording process where, offering subtext to the blood and thunder of most of the music, the teachings of Meher Baba about each individual being as a water drop in the ocean of Oneness found expression not only in watery imagery—rain and sea—but also the story's conclusion as Jimmy, confused and disillusioned, takes off in a boat to a rock, there to end his life or find wisdom, bringing the album to an end on a deliberately ambiguous note.

The biggest headache during recording was the quad concept. The record and hi-fi industry were trying to launch quadrophonic sound reproduction—that is, music coming from four speakers rather than stereo's two or mono's one. Pete, of course, loved the idea of *Quadrophenia* being a sonic pioneer, but in the event found quad technology over-hyped and unworkable and abandoned that aspect of making the record.

Nor was the four-way split of Jimmy's character adequately expressed, as became clear when the record came out. So, in both respects, the "quad" parts of *Quadrophenia* were more talk than delivery.

But behind the scenes, two of the four parts were asserting themselves against a third. Where *Tommy* was very much a collaborative effort and had included songs by John—"Cousin Kevin" and "Fiddle About"—because Pete had found their subjects of child abuse too painful to write songs about himself, *Quadrophenia* was from first to last written by Pete, who, with engineer Ron Nevison, had produced the whole album, right down to its myriad sound effects from demo to finished product. Roger and John, however, had by now made their own solo albums and felt their views on the final mix were informed enough to warrant more serious consideration than they got. Roger hated the echo effect used on his voice as well as the lack of the album's sonic variety, and John deplored his brass parts' lack of definition in a sound picture of complex density. During rehearsals to take *Quadrophenia* on the road, tensions boiled over when Pete, hurt by Roger's griping, swung at him with his guitar, receiving in return an uppercut that knocked him out cold.

FALLOUT SHELTER
The Who
North American Tour
1973

TOP: December 9, 1972: *Tommy* performers Maggie Bell, Roger, and Richie Havens in conversation with producer Lou Reizner.

ABOVE: The US tour poster, 1973.

OPPOSITE: December 9, 1972: *Tommy* on stage with Sandy Denny, Graham Bell, and Roger.

Frustration and Fury

This being the Who, these problems were not concealed from the fans in media interviews. One reason for the intense bond the fans felt for the Who was the way that they were taken into the band's confidence, sharing their problems as well as high hopes. That intense bond paid off in huge advance sales of a very expensive double album, lavishly illustrated with a photo book by Ethan Russell storyboarding what happens to Jimmy in the course of the album's narrative in grainy, evocative monochrome. Ticket sales were also phenomenal, with vast lines forming at venue box offices in the days before computer ticketing, never mind the Internet. But where *Tommy* was very simple to play live, growing in power in live performance, *Quadrophenia* had two problems.

The first was sonic: the synth parts were integral to several songs but synth technology had not reached the point where the parts could be programmed and played live, so the Who fell back on backing tapes. This forced them to play in strict time, where their live practice for years had been about push and pull and taking off in the moment. Worse, it forced them to rely on machines working reliably, including the signal in Keith's headphones (which obstructed his freeform performing style) to synch him in. At a show in Newcastle that November, there was a tape glitch and Keith came in fifteen seconds too early; Pete went mad, trashed the tapes and a guitar, and stormed offstage. Would the show go on? Without tapes, the *Quadrophenia* segment had to be abandoned, and the Who found themselves playing a greatest-hits set instead.

The other problem, more pronounced in North America, was *Quadrophenia*'s subject matter. Mods were a purely British—and mostly London—youth movement, so Pete felt each song from the new album needed an explanatory preamble, and Roger agreed. That meant sacrificing momentum, and

John in particular was irritated by how the band's natural stage energy was dissipated by between-song talk, while the fans grew restless.

Then there were the personal issues. Such were the problems with *Quadrophenia* and feeling let down by Kit and Chris that Pete was hitting the brandy, thus shortening his fuse. Keith's wife Kim, meanwhile, could no longer cope with her husband's escalating drink and pill problem, and left him, throwing him into an even worse state. (Kim would soon enter into a lifelong relationship with Faces keyboardist Ian "Mac" McLagan, neither the first nor last time the fates of the Who and their fellow former mod rockers would overlap.)

Less than a fortnight after Newcastle, at the Cow Palace in San Francisco, Keith's drink was spiked with animal tranquillizer and he passed out halfway through "Won't Get Fooled Again." He was revived after a fifteen-minute break, only to collapse again in "Magic Bus," at which point Pete asked if there were any drummers in the audience. Nineteen-year-old Scott Halpin volunteered and found himself on Keith's kit to end the show with "Naked Eye." Undaunted, two weeks later in

Montreal, Keith initiated a comprehensive hotel suite trashing, and Pete gleefully joined in. The Mounties broke up the party and hauled band and touring party (save early-to-bed Roger) to spend the night in the cells.

For all the problems, tensions, and excess, some nights found the Who on fire, such as that December at the Philadelphia Spectrum. But the band were dropping more and more *Quadrophenia* numbers from the set, as they felt it simply was not taking off with fans. With the band not fully supporting the album live, as they had done for *Tommy*, it began to slip down the charts. To Pete, *Quadrophenia* felt like a flop, though only compared to *Tommy*. Yet it would continue to see and be seen by many fans as the Who's greatest masterpiece, especially after it was made into a hit movie six years later.

Tommy never needed a movie to have its masterpiece status secured. But it got one anyway—again, six years after the album. *Tommy*—the all-star, singing, dancing movie—served to camouflage a band hitting the age of thirty and struggling to keep it together.

ABOVE: The cast of *Tommy* at the Rainbow Theatre, London, December 9, 1972. From left: Merry Clayton, Richie Havens, Peter Sellers, Sandy Denny, Graham Bell (holding paper), Roger, Pete, John, and Keith.

chapter 13

Rock Gods under Pressure

FROM THE START, Kit Lambert had seen himself as a filmmaker who had allowed himself to be derailed into becoming a band manager, creative Svengali, and covisionary of the rock opera form, succeeding where his father Constant had failed in combining high art with the people's music of America.

After he spent years trying to realize *Tommy* for the big screen, the irony is that when it finally happened, Kit was out of the picture, having wearied even the loyal Pete both by his increasingly unglued behavior and evidence of his skimming income that should have gone to the musicians.

His departure cast a further shadow over Pete, whose drinking was getting heavier and beginning to cloud his marriage, as Keith's had before, the pair now forming a bond over the bottle despite Pete's gloomy doubts about the band, their audience, and his own creative direction—a contrast to Keith's reckless affability and recoil from introspection.

LEFT: At last, *Tommy* the movie, starring Roger, 1975.

Also stressing Pete was the task of taking *Tommy* to the screen. So possessive had Kit been about the opera he felt to be as much his as the Who's that he had hindered rather than hastened it to the screen when there was no shortage of offers. At last there came an offer from a man whom Pete and the rest of the band trusted, and things moved quickly. Robert Stigwood, whose Reaction Records had thrown the Who a lifeline in 1966, was the impresario who put it all together. For stars, he insisted on a cameo from Hollywood's hippest male lead, Jack Nicholson, and a former leading lady of Elvis' movie career, Ann-Margret. Playing a big role

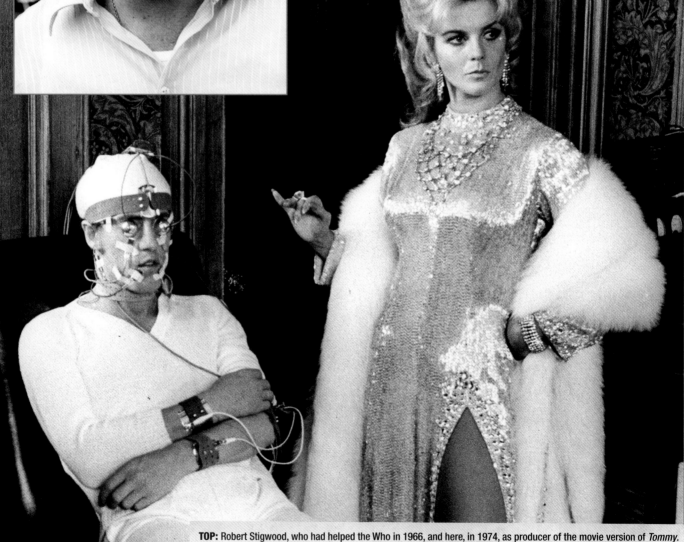

TOP: Robert Stigwood, who had helped the Who in 1966, and here, in 1974, as producer of the movie version of *Tommy.*

ABOVE: Ann-Margret, who played Tommy's mother, with Roger as Tommy.

TOP: Ann-Margret as Tommy's mother and Oliver Reed as his stepfather in the movie version of *Tommy*.

ABOVE: Oliver Reed hams up the villainy.

as Tommy's "Uncle" Frank would be the British star Oliver Reed, who shot to stardom in the controversial movies *Women in Love* and *The Devils*, directed by classical music buff Ken Russell, who agreed to helm *Tommy* after hearing Reizner's orchestrated version. A director of great sensitivity to music as well as bold, even bombastic vision, he shared with Pete the Wagnerian instinct for the total, overwhelming artwork, and the pair inspired each other, though arguably to a finished movie long on glitter, glamour, energy, and splash but short on subtle shades and deeper resonance.

Pete agreed to Ken's demands that the story follow World War II rather than I, that Tommy should witness his father's murder, and that, as in the Wagnerian operatic tradition, there would be no dialogue, the story being told through the songs, which would need to be revised and rerecorded with vocal performances from the cast. Aside from the actors—and Nicholson turned out to be a creditable crooner—musicians such as Pete's friend and Stigwood client Eric Clapton performed, as did Arthur Brown. The biggest star was Elton John—then at the height of his superstardom, selling around one in fifty of every album bought worldwide—playing the Pinball Wizard. During six weeks at Ramport, Pete re-created *Tommy* in the big, bright, colorful style of Elton's huge hit albums—a far cry from the dense, tense, and often dark music of *Quadrophenia*, recorded less than a year before.

Missing from the lineup was Keith, then away reprising his role as madcap drummer J. D. Clover in *That'll Be the Day*'s sequel, *Stardust*.

TOP: Roger with director Ken Russell on location on England's South Coast for *Tommy*, June 1974.

ABOVE: Roger as Tommy, with Paul Nicholas as Cousin Kevin.

RIGHT: Keith with David Essex, Billy Fury, and the other stars of the 1973 rock movie *That'll Be the Day*.

OPPOSITE: Pete supporting his old pal Eric Clapton's cameo in the movie *Tommy*.

Bereft that his wife and daughter had left him, then
hit hard by the death of his father, Keith took off
for Los Angeles with his new girlfriend Annette
Walter-Lax and joined a coterie of rock stars
partying hard to forget their troubles, among them
his pal Ringo, John Lennon, and Harry Nilsson.
Playing drums instead on the *Tommy* soundtrack
was Face (and former Small Face) Kenney Jones.
Five years later, it would turn out to be a significant
substitution.

Roger, of course, would star as Tommy, making
him a movie star when it came out.

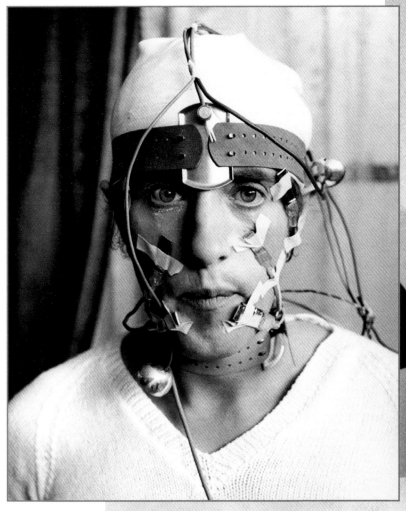

ABOVE: Roger wired up as Tommy.

RIGHT: Elton John played the Pinball Wizard in the movie *Tommy*.

The Who Hold Down the Fort

But during the course of making the movie, the legal issues with Kit and Chris as both the Who's managers and—in a clear conflict of interest—owners of the their record label, Track, resulted in the freezing of a lot of the band's income from record sales until matters were resolved.

As a band where each individual had a lavish lifestyle to maintain—Pete was now buying boats—and as employers of a loyal team of managers, technicians, and assistants, the Who needed to keep the money rolling in, and playing live was their best generator of ready cash. The stage was also where the band bonded, and Pete realized that—with Roger making a solo musical career as a pop star for himself and clearly taking to screen acting, with John also making solo records, and with Keith partying hard in Lotus Land (L.A.)—the Who were drifting apart.

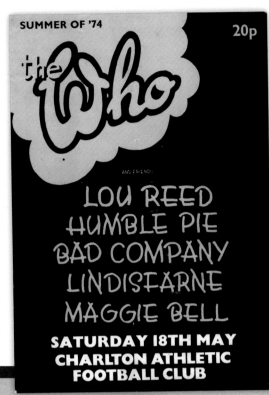

SUMMER OF '74   20p

the Who

AND FRIENDS

LOU REED
HUMBLE PIE
BAD COMPANY
LINDISFARNE
MAGGIE BELL

**SATURDAY 18TH MAY
CHARLTON ATHLETIC
FOOTBALL CLUB**

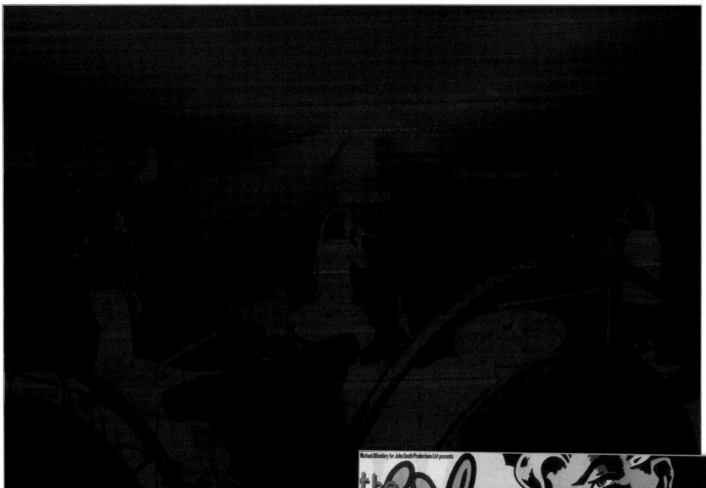

Playing some dates as the Who was vital from several points of view. As a live act, they were getting bigger and bigger, in Europe headlining huge outdoor venues, as they could in the United States. The biggest show they played in 1974 was in front of eighty thousand fans that May at the Valley, home of London's Charlton Athletic, the soccer club for which new Who manager Bill Curbishley's brother Alan played. With the crowd far surpassing the official limit, the show was good but not great, Pete being on a pre-birthday bender. The following month, the Who played four nights in New York's Madison Square Garden, shows where Pete felt confronted by fans who wanted only the classic Who experience and would not allow change or progress.

TOP: The Who open the Parc des Expositions, Paris, on February 10, 1974. Such was the crush outside that the doors had to be opened eight hours early and the crowd far exceeded the official limit.

ABOVE: Poster for the Who's big 1974 London outdoor headliner; for the event, Dave Mason was replaced by Maggie Bell.

OPPOSITE TOP: The program for the Who's big 1974 London outdoor headliner.

OPPOSITE BOTTOM: Roger's climactic moment in *Tommy*, the movie.

That his colleague's heart was palpably not in it infuriated Roger, who in interviews laid the blame for any recent performance shortcomings at the door of Pete and his drinking. Not shy of airing their differences in public, the Who were letting the fans get a closer look into their world than any other group of rock superstars, but the impression they were getting was that the band, once again, could fall apart at any moment.

A year on from the release of *Quadrophenia*, the Who had released nothing new, though they had been hard at work recording a new version of *Tommy* for the movie. To have an album out for the valuable Christmas market and to beat the boot-leggers who had been selling sloppily mixed and mastered rare Who material to hardcore fans, John busied himself assembling *Odds & Sods*, an album of orphan tracks. Spanning a decade of recording and including such *Lifehouse* outtakes as "Pure and

Easy" and "Naked Eye," the High Numbers' "I'm the Face," and the starting point for 1972's quickly abandoned *Rock Is Dead—Long Live Rock!* project, "Long Live Rock!," the collection presented the Who as stylistic quick-change artists and was far from a smooth listening experience. Yet this album of mis-fits and rejects sold well, commercially holding the fort and confirming the band's superstar status.

ABOVE: Restless at the Who's studio and with live inactivity, John overdid his solo career, to diminishing returns.

TOP RIGHT: The 1974 compilation album *Odds & Sods*...

BOTTOM RIGHT: ...with its spin-off single, "Long Live Rock."

At this point, convinced of the Who's Midas touch, their US record company, MCA, which had absorbed Decca, made a terrible mistake: it bankrolled a Keith Moon album to the tune of $200,000—around three times the cost of making the original *Tommy*, itself considered expensive at the time. At a time when numerous great rock talents were losing their way in L.A. in a non-stop party of coke, booze, and groupies, the all-star *Two Sides of the Moon* set a new high for waste and awfulness. Deciding to sing rather than drum (save on three songs), Keith sincerely butchered Beatles and Beach Boys classics, assisted by Ringo Starr, Harry Nilsson, David Bowie, Joe Walsh of the Eagles, Jim Keltner, Bobby Keys, Klaus Voorman, John Sebastian, Flo & Eddie, Spencer Davis, and surf legend Dick Dale. Released in March 1975 to embarrassing sales, it only proved that Who fans were loyal but not stupid. No more successful was John's 1974 third album, titled *Rigor Mortis Sets In*, which offered fans fair warning of what would prove John's artistic and commercial nadir, his 1975 follow-up *Mad Dog*. Restless and unable to resist the lure of the road, he compounded these follies by going on tour in the UK and United States with his band Ox, losing a fortune from poor ticket sales. John would not make another solo album until 1981.

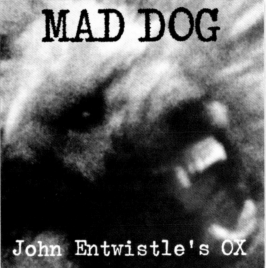

ABOVE: *That'll Be the Day* star Keith and his buddy Ringo Starr at the movie's 1973 West Coast premiere, with fellow carouser, the singer-songwriter Harry Nilsson.

RIGHT (from top): Keith's solo album was a catastrophic folly, while John's mid-'70s efforts ran out of inspiration.

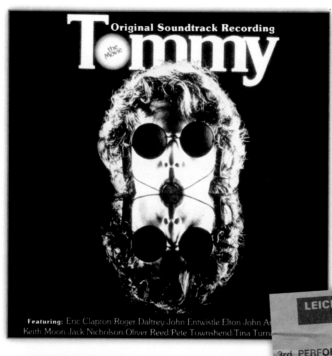

TOP and ABOVE: *Tommy*, the 1975 movie soundtrack album, UK advertising poster, and ticket (inset).

ABOVE RIGHT: Roger's *Ride a Rock Horse* solo album.

RIGHT: Roger in his second starring role for the movie *Lisztomania*.

OPPOSITE: Poster for the movie *Lisztomania*.

LISZTOMANIA

Roger, on the other hand, was on a roll. Impressed by his acting talent in *Tommy*, director Ken Russell cast him as the piano virtuoso and composer Franz Liszt in his next movie, *Lisztomania*, which extravagantly reimagined the nineteenth-century Romantic icon's career as if a modern rock star, with the Pope played by Ringo. During breaks in filming, Roger recorded his second solo album, *Ride a Rock Horse*, whose cover depicted him as a bare-chested centaur and was released to commercial success in July '75, three months after the release of the *Tommy* movie, which topped the US box office for a week and made the Who—and Roger in particular—stars way outside their loyal fan base.

Pete's Private Hell

Many Who loyalists felt the movie (and correspondingly popular soundtrack album) was a travesty, a tacky big-budget celebration of celebrity and hubris, and not really what the band were about. Strangest of all, Pete was party to it all. Still feeling needlessly rejected after *Quadrophenia* had not repeated either in record sales or live performance the overwhelming success of *Tommy*, Pete was coming to believe his boldest, most complex, and progressive artistic statements were going over the heads of an increasingly conservative fan base. For Pete, rebooting *Tommy* meant simply giving the people what they wanted out of the Who—bombast and empty spectacle. Drinking hard, demoralized, and questioning the point of carrying on with the Who except out of loyalty to his bandmates, Pete was writing songs with no big picture in view save to reflect what was on his mind.

It wasn't all gloom, however. The previous August, Pete and Keith had made a few cameo appearances on Eric Clapton's US tour. After struggling with heroin addiction, the blues-rock guitar god had been helped to start his recovery by Pete and now returned to the music scene, finding renewed popularity as an easy-going, tasteful interpreter of blues, vintage rock, and reggae songs rather than as the incendiary virtuoso who had made his name in the late '60s. There was a lesson there for Pete: it didn't all have to be full on.

Feeling profoundly tired and short of inspiration, Pete presented thirty songs in a variety of styles to Roger, hoping to mend bridges by giving him a free hand choosing which to sing on the next Who album. Pete was surprised when Roger tended to the darker, more personal songs—but then,

ABOVE RIGHT: John's band, Ox, ended up losing him money.

OPPOSITE: Pete mid-windmill at the Ahoy in Rotterdam, Netherlands, October 27, 1975.

despite his growing stardom outside the Who, Roger was angry with Keith and Pete's drinking, and Pete's pessimism about the band stultifying into an oldies act just as he, now thirty, was clearly no longer young either. Unfocused and drifting, the band for the first time let themselves be distracted during the recording—which Glyn Johns worked hard to produce, such was the lack of focus and energy—just as their friends the Faces had seldom done themselves full justice in the studio thanks to a patchy work ethic but substantial play ethic. Former Face and fellow Meher Baba follower Ronnie Lane had encouraged Pete that a bouncy folk-style song of mild innuendo, "Squeeze Box," was a great single.

No less throwaway was the cover design and title of the ensuing album, *The Who by Numbers*, its cover art being a join-the-dots pen-and-ink caricature of the band by John Entwistle—an even more flip visualization of a flip title than the urination-on-an-obelisk of *Who's Next*. At least it was cheap, costing £32, as distinct from the £16,000 (around $37,000 at the time) to create *Quadrophenia*'s photo book and packaging.

Released in October 1975, *The Who by Numbers* immediately stood out for containing far more nakedly autobiographical songs—in particular the self-lacerating "However Much I Booze," "How Many Friends," and "Dreaming from the Waist"—than any previous record by the Who, or indeed by virtually any other rock band of the day. As raw and pained as the most introspective work by John Lennon, it was short on power chords and mania but long on self-pity, even self-disgust. Glyn Johns had wrung listenable, even exhilarating performances from the band, but there was little to get fists pumping; "Slip Kid" was perhaps the only number that might have made the grade on *Who's Next*. Though critics were intrigued at this insight into Pete's private hell and saluted him for his honesty, the fans greeted it politely rather than enthusiastically.

ABOVE: The single "Squeeze Box" and its host album *The Who by Numbers*.
RIGHT: The Who get ready to hit the stage in June 1976.

ABOVE: As the '70s wore on, Keith, Pete, and John partied to the point of self-destruction.

LEFT and INSET: 1976 Munich gig poster; 1975 concert ticket.

OPPOSITE (clockwise from top left): *The Story of the Who* compilation album; 1976 Oakland gig poster with the Grateful Dead; and tour programs from 1975–76, including *Bellboy* with a centerfold of Keith.

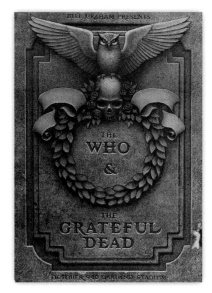

Nothing damped fans' enthusiasm for seeing the Who live, though; for the energy, tension, and release of their performances, they could credibly claim to top even the Stones and Led Zeppelin and now the new star, Bruce Springsteen, while some fans feared that if they didn't see them now, the chance may be lost for good.

Recommitting himself to the band for now, and despite his anxiety that the band's monstrously loud P.A. was further damaging his hearing, Pete got back into the swing of things. The wildly oversubscribed shows were, according to John, the best the band ever played, despite a set list leaning backward heavily toward *Tommy*, the old hits, and the *Who's Next* blockbusters. Novelties included the first (and by modern standard very tentative) use as a visual effect of lasers, and Roger's T-shirt proclaiming "George Davis Is Innocent," in reference to the recent conviction for armed robbery of a career criminal based on extremely questionable police evidence. (He was released the following year.)

A measure of the Who's standing as a live act at that point was the record-breaking audience of seventy-eight thousand fans they drew to Detroit's Pontiac Silver Dome—the largest ever indoor rock concert, the venue's size requiring what was back then a major innovation, a huge video screen to show the action to faraway fans. And the dates continued through most of 1976 in both the UK and North America, spanning huge outdoor sports stadiums, including Charlton again, as well as arenas. On October 21, 1976, the Who finally came off the road after a show in Toronto. No one knew that it would be the last time the band would play before a paying audience with Keith Moon.

chapter 14

Battling through Tragedy

THOUGH HE WOULD RALLY from time to time, get fit, and play with all his old brilliance, Keith was visibly sliding. Roger and John felt strongly that, though touring offered Keith endless opportunities for excess and self-destruction, he was quite capable of raising hell anywhere, and at least when he was on the road his bandmates and the Who's roadies could keep an eye on him. Keith tried to detox in 1976 but lacked the commitment to stick with it, and over the next two years would swing between ever more bizarre behavior in L.A., including biting his movie-star-next-door-neighbor Steve McQueen's dog, amid attempts to put the brakes on his alcohol, cocaine, and pill habit.

LEFT: Keith on stage at the Ahoy in Rotterdam, Netherlands, on October 27, 1975. He was approaching his live swansong.

Pete, meanwhile, wearied by years of working virtually nonstop on Who albums, tours, and the *Tommy* movie, was feeling disenchanted with what he felt was less a vehicle for his expanding spiritual and artistic energies than a treadmill of increasingly narrow-minded fan expectations. Behind the scenes, too, he was dismayed to find he had misplaced his trust in the straight dealing of Kit, Chris, and others on the business and management side. His gloom and self-absorption was not helping his marriage, and spending more and more time messing about on boats only partly cheered him up.

Pete did enjoy the company of former (Small) Face Ronnie Lane, and, with Glyn Johns producing, the pair of Baba followers collaborated on a folk-inflected album called *Rough Mix*; among the many guest players was session keyboardist John "Rabbit" Bundrick. A hard-drinking Texan, Bundrick hit it off with Pete, who felt he was a new musical foil.

ABOVE: Incoming keyboard player John "Rabbit" Bundrick and friend, 1979.
RIGHT: The Who show signs of wear and tear, stress and strain, 1978.

But while *Rough Mix* was a good record by two big stars, it sold only respectfully when released in September 1977. That was the year when the previous year's growing of rumor of a new music and youth movement called punk exploded into the mainstream in Britain and transformed the landscape.

Of the five British bands particularly breaking through from the start of 1977, four—the Sex Pistols, the Clash, the Damned, and the Jam—owed almost everything to what the Who had last been twelve years prior. If Pete was feeling the Who were stuck in a rut of fans' conservatism and his own premature midlife crisis, here was proof that the Who had got it amazingly right for a while, even if a new generation was keen to seize the baton whether they wanted to give it up or not.

With rock's future as the soundtrack to rebel youth in new hands, Pete felt more than ever that the Who needed to present their inspirational past. There was a project in hand supervised by a fan called Jeff Stein who was trawling through archives in search of vintage screen footage. With the Who providing a $300,000 budget, he would also be shooting scenes with the band live and as individuals for a documentary to be titled *The Kids Are Alright*. A night fly as well as a madman, Keith's sequences swallowed more than his share of time and budget.

TOP LEFT: *Rough Mix*, Pete's album with former Small Face and Face, Ronnie Lane.

LEFT: Pete with the Who at Madison Square Garden, New York, on November 3, 1976.

OPPOSITE: With the 1978 release of their career-surveying movie, *The Kids Are Alright*, the Who recalled their past, as here, from 1971.

The Godfather of Punk

Meanwhile, challenged by punk—of which he was hailed by the highly influential UK music press as "Godfather"—Pete was writing fresh songs, seeking an integration between the ever-more complex and cerebral "old wave," of which he was a part, and the honest, back-to-basics new wave, of which he was a forerunner. After a night on the tiles with the Sex Pistols when, after a collapsing in a Soho doorway, he was sent on his way home by a policeman who recognized him, he wrote the song of rueful self-disgust and cryptic romantic/spiritual redemption that would title the band's album, "Who Are You."

The introspective vein that Pete started on *The Who by Numbers* continued because his situation had not fundamentally changed: no longer in his twenties, with his marriage growing stale, challenged by younger acts, and struggling with the diverging agendas of his colleagues no longer ready to follow blindly his creative lead.

Though Roger's third solo album, *One of the Boys*, boasted the talents of, among others, Paul McCartney, Eric Clapton, Colin Blunstone, Rod Argent, Mick Ronson, and the Who's John and Keith, it had the casual air of a hobbyist's side project and only loyalists invested on its release in the summer of '77. Though Rogermania had clearly peaked, the singer now demanded to pick and choose from Pete's songbook, so Pete had to work hard writing and demoing numbers from which Roger would make his selection.

In the event, Roger did not shun Pete's songs of self-analysis, in which, as on "New Song," Pete not only admitted to repeating himself and running on fumes creatively but also pointed out that the fans seemed happy with that. Among the old wave "rock dinosaurs," the Who retained a special place in part for their past achievements but also for acknowledging that the new wave had rebooted the game, as on "Music Must Change." But if anyone expected the band to revert to the terse, three-minute, three-chord manic rock songs of 1965, they would be disappointed.

ABOVE: Roger exposed, performing on stage, New York, 1977.

RIGHT: Roger's 1977 underwhelming solo album, *One of the Boys*.

OPPOSITE: Hailed as the Godfather of Punk, Pete was intrigued by the new rock movement and built alliances, such as with Siouxsie Sioux of Siouxsie & the Banshees.

The band's most synthesizer-dominated album yet, *Who Are You* was also their least viscerally exciting and most thoughtful-sounding, with most of its songs addressing the predicament of being Pete of the Who in the late '70s.

The recording of the album was efficient rather than inspired, though Pete recalls Roger coming to blows—and possibly a headbutt—with producer Glyn Johns, who quit the sessions to be replaced by Pete's brother-in-law, the engineer Jon Astley. Invited to audition to play keyboards, Pete's new pal John "Rabbit" Bundrick was accepted but made the mistake of going out for a few drinks with Keith, the upshot being an altercation with a cab

driver in which his hand was broken, so ruling him out of the band for the time being. Keith, seriously out of condition and struggling to play with his old skill and fire, often had to be worked around when, in the past, his energy would drive everyone forward.

Aside from Pete's extreme reluctance to tour, Keith was clearly in no shape to do so. In December 1977, the Who had convened to play a small free show in London's Kilburn for Jeff Stein's documentary; the band, and Keith especially, were so ring-rusty that the live footage was almost unusable, and now, five months later, wearing the same stage clothes for continuity reasons, the band had to have another, better go at Shepperton Film Studios, just outside London.

Keith clearly had problems with alcoholism and drug addiction, and they were only leading in one direction. His friends in the band, though utterly exasperated by his irresponsibility, were helping as best they could. The key problem was that Keith

ABOVE: Who fans form a line for the first hearing of *Who Are You* at the Palladium, New York, in August 1979.

TOP LEFT: The single "Who Are You."

LEFT: April 1, 1977: Roger in Battersea, London, a short walk from the Who's Ramport Studios.

OPPOSITE: John and Roger with the Who at Madison Square Garden, New York, on November 3, 1976.

was spending more and more time out of reach, in Malibu, California, hanging out and burning through money he had not yet earned. Back in London, he was put in charge of various Who businesses in the hope it would give him something constructive to do, and the promotional machine swung into gear to push the first album of new Who songs to be released in almost three years.

Released on August 18, 1978, *Who Are You* shot up the US charts in particular but did slightly less well in the UK, where many of the band's younger fans had defected to punk, feeling that they could now get what they needed from the likes of the Clash and devoted Who-'65 stylists the Jam. Keith was in London, working on overdubs for *The Kids Are Alright*; he was doing his best, but the energy was ebbing. By way of an omen, the band's old manager, Peter Meaden, virtually penniless after years of addiction, died at his parents' home of a barbiturate overdose on July 29.

The Worst Happens

On September 7, Keith and Annette Walter-Lax, now engaged, were invited by his old pal Paul McCartney to the start of Buddy Holly Week, on what would have been the rock pioneer's forty-third birthday, at London's Peppermint Park restaurant, where they shared a booth with Paul and his wife, Linda, and former Faces drummer Kenney Jones. They then went on to the midnight screening premier of the Gary Busey movie *The Buddy Holly Story*

Uncharacteristically tired and subdued, Keith made his excuses early, and he and Annette returned to the flat in Mayfair's very plush Curzon Place he was renting from his L.A. pal Harry Nilsson—the very same flat in which Mama Cass

ABOVE: September 6, 1978: Keith's last night out, with his girlfriend Annette Walter-Lax at the film premiere of *The Buddy Holly Story* in London.

LEFT: The *Who Are You* album.

OPPOSITE: Only John could raise a smile as the unhappy band publicize the *Who Are You* album.

Elliot of the Mamas & the Papas had died four years earlier. Annette cooked Keith lamb cutlets and they watched a movie, *The Abominable Dr. Phibes*, in bed until about 4 a.m. Keith then took some Heminevrin (chlormethiazole, a sedative used in treating and preventing symptoms of acute alcohol withdrawal) and went to sleep.

Keith woke at 7:30 a.m. and asked Annette to cook him his usual steak breakfast. He watched some more TV and, unbeknown to Annette, swallowed more Heminevrin. They slept through the day—Annette on the couch because of Keith's snoring—and when she went in check on him at 3:40 p.m. he was lying face down, not breathing. Trying in vain to revive him, Annette called the emergency services, but it was far too late. Pete was in the studio that day when Roger phoned: "He's done it." No more need be said.

At the age of thirty-two, Keith had died of a massive overdose, but the coroner found no evidence of suicidal intent; possessed of a seemingly superhuman tolerance to pills, Keith had simply assumed there was no upper limit. But there was.

The Who had been drifting apart for years. Pete was disillusioned with being a spokesman for the rock generation that had now left youth far behind and found a new set of anxieties. Getting

TOP: The new Who rock London's Wembley Stadium on August 18, 1979.

ABOVE: Mourners at Keith's funeral at the Golders Green Crematorium, London.

the first whistles of tinnitus, he dreaded returning to the stage and, indeed, had refused to tour *Who Are You* (which, in the wake of Keith's headline-news death, was selling better than ever). With Ronnie Lane, he now had a creative outlet more suited to his spiritual condition and ageing temperament than the Who; he had opened a bookshop, too, and loved his boat and growing children.

Yet it was Pete, the least committed member of the band, who, having issued a public statement mourning the loss of their irreplaceable drummer, called a meeting with Roger and John and persuaded them that the band owed it to Keith to carry on—with a replacement. That replacement, Pete urged, should be the cool, reliable, and far from excessive or zany Kenney Jones—who was, of course, one of the last people to see Keith alive.

Years later, Pete put his utterly perverse decision to fly in the face of his own drift to a midlife solo career down to shock and grief, with Roger and John too shocked themselves to resist. Bit by bit, Pete repented of his decision, but he felt he could not back out. Roger saw it as another evolutionary stage in a band that had, after all, been in existence for some years before Keith joined. As well as Kenney taking Keith's place, that evolution could also include an unofficial fifth member, and one who was not only not a west Londoner but also not even a Brit: at Pete's behest, and with his hand now healed, John "Rabbit" Bundrick joined the Who.

Though Pete felt that Rabbit was impulsive, drank too much, and told crazy stories, he also believed he played the Hammond organ as well as Billy Preston, and there could be no higher praise. Nor was he the only one to think so, the thirty-two-year-old Houston-born keyboardist having recorded with numerous artists on the UK's prestigious Island label, including blues-rockers Free, folk-rockers John Martyn and Sandy Denny,

and, on the albums that introduced him to the rock crowd, the reggae legend Bob Marley. Record producer Glyn Johns rated him very highly, and it was he who had introduced him to Pete—who, two years later, introduced him to the Chicago crowd as "a new friend for me . . . a right c***, a toe-rag, a piss artist, a shit bag. He's also a genius."

That show in December 1979 took place just five days after a tragedy that ended the year on a terrible note.

It had all seemed to be going so well. Cheered that with Rabbit in the group the band could now play live some of the songs that never could have made it to the stage before, and that in Kenney they had a solid pro behind the kit who would not cause problems, Pete agreed to go along with Roger and John's hunger to tour after what amounted

ABOVE: The movie *Quadrophenia*, featuring Sting of the Police (left) with Phil Daniels (center) and Lesley Ash (right) in the lead roles.

to nearly three years away from live performance. Fans who had seen the band before had to get used to Kenney's solid tempo and utter lack of explosiveness. Roger (newly shorn, new wave–style), Pete, and John were their usual selves, though, and fans were more than willing to give the Who 2.0 more than just a chance but a rapturous welcome.

Meet the New Who

The band had a following wind with the release that year of two movies celebrating their work. Jeff Stein's *The Kids Are Alright* came out in June, its timing proving a memorial to the Who 1.0 with Keith, who had died a week after seeing its rough cut. Years before MTV, never mind YouTube and archive video clips on demand, it was a revelation for fans, showing material either never seen before or not since first screened years previously.

ABOVE: *The Kids Are Alright* soundtrack album.

RIGHT: Pete with Anna Nicholas and Allan Love, stars of the London stage production of *Tommy* that opened in early 1979.

Its soundtrack album of live material spanning the years from 1965 to 1978 did particularly well in the United States, selling over a million copies in a few months.

No less significant, six years after the release of the *Quadrophenia* album, the project made it to the screen as directed by Franc Roddam who, like many leading British movie directors of the time, came from a background in TV commercials. Fleshing out the narrative, he also cast several unknowns in key parts, for many of whom this was the start of successful acting careers. Playing the cameo role of the Ace Face in silver mohair suit was not an actor but a musician who was just breaking into the big time on his own account with a new wave/reggae fusion trio called the Police: Sting. Most successful in the UK, where there

QUADROPHENIA

THE WHO Songs from Quadrophenia • Original Soundtrack

DIE ROCKER GEGEN DIE MODS... DIE MODS GEGEN DIE ROCKER... VEREINT GEGEN DIE BULLEN...

QUADROPHENIA

DIE STORY EINER GENERATION

TOP: *Quadrophenia* with Sting of the Police as the Ace Face.

ABOVE: The *Quadrophenia* soundtrack album.

RIGHT: The German *Quadrophenia* movie poster.

OPPOSITE TOP: Pete engaging in some British seaside cuisine with *Quadrophenia* star Phil Daniels.

OPPOSITE BOTTOM: *Quadrophenia* star Lesley Ash braves the Brighton breezes.

was a growing mod-revival scene focused on the Jam, punky devotees of the Who, Small Faces, and mid-'60s pop art, the film *Quadrophenia* became essential viewing. Likewise, in its echo of the 1964 mod scene, it presciently anticipated the '80s in its portrayal of youthful tribalism, obsession with the right fashion brands so as not to be left behind, and the common reality of low-paid, dead-end jobs. Also featuring mod favorites from the '60s, the soundtrack album offered a selection of original 1973 album tracks remixed by John, plus three inferior songs that seemed to fit, newly recorded with Kenney.

On their 1979 tour, which included five nights at Madison Square Garden and stadium shows at the Pontiac Silver Dome and Wembley, London, the band added a brass section part way through, and all seemed to be going well. But tragedy struck on December 3, at the Riverfront Coliseum in Cincinnati. Because most of the seating for the eighteen thousand sellout capacity was unassigned, first-come, first-served, thousands of fans had arrived early and lined up outside up in freezing conditions. Inside, the band decided to do a late soundcheck, and, hearing it and thinking the

performance had started, the fans outside rushed to get in. In the ensuing stampede, eleven fans died, with twenty-three injured. Fearing that canceling the show would cause further fan havoc, the decision was made not to tell the band what had happened until afterward.

The Who soldiered on to complete the tour, rallying their mood within a few days when they reached Chicago and then Philadelphia to play long, eclectic encores. After playing the benefit Concert for Kampuchea in London at the end of the year, the band rested for three months before returning to the road in Europe. Maybe by working through the pain, the '80s would see the Who bounce back to high spirits. It was not to be.

ABOVE: New boy Kenney Jones brings up the rear.

LEFT: *The Kids Are Alright* movie poster.

OPPOSITE: *Quadrophenia* with Sting on the Brighton seafront; his monogrammed scooter bears the initials of his real name, Gordon Sumner.

chapter 15

Burn Out!

AFTER A SHOW AT THE ZÜRICH, Hallenstadion in March 1980, Pete had a cocaine withdrawal crisis, as he told the author a few years later: "I became so utterly disenchanted with the Who. They really were pathetic in their last days—a dire, shadowy, awful, moneymaking desolate dinosaur. Dinosaur is just too high a term. Just fucking awful. But they were good fun to be with—there were good people in and around the band.

"Nonetheless, it was a dispiriting experience playing this tired set of songs—this set that advertisers insist on being played on American radio stations because they were the only fucking songs people would respond to. We'd given up on our own history. So we just trotted out 'Baba O'Riley,' 'Won't Get Fooled Again,' 'Who Are You,' 'Pinball Wizard,' 'My Generation,' and dragged them out to six-minutes each, so we'd be playing maybe ten songs in a two-hour show, and at the end it would be a half-hour version of 'Summertime Blues.' It was just miserable for me as a musician who likes to write new songs and hear decent music.

LEFT: Back to their sullen, purposeful mid-'60s image, except for new boy Kenney Jones (far left), who fails to get with the program.

"One day, after a show in some big Swiss town, I just couldn't stand it anymore, so I took a car to Berne, checked into a hotel, but just couldn't be comfortable there. So I had this old army greatcoat, a bottle of brandy, and a Swiss army knife, and I went into Berne and started to walk from about eleven o'clock at night to about five in the morning. I hopped over a fence and found this bunch of caves, where I went to sleep. Next day I got up and was brushing myself down, and a guy on a bridge shouted you must get out of there. I thought he must have thought I was a tramp. So I went back to the hotel and said what are those caves? And he said, 'Those are the famous bear pits of Berne!' I said, 'But there weren't any bears!'

"I could have died! Torn to pieces. What a great way to go! I was going through this nihilistic, suicidal period and I felt really, really cheated. I felt my destiny was to live, and it was very irritating!"

Yet two days later, the band played in Vienna as scheduled, Pete self-obliviating with brandy and cocaine as the tour continued over the Atlantic until mid-July, running through the Midwest, Canada, and the western and Southern US states. The following year, the Who took it easy, with only two months of dates in the United States and Europe, one London show in February 1981 becoming a shambles thanks to Pete's consumption of four bottles of brandy followed by a fight with Roger. Five weeks later, though, they released their first album since *Who Are You.*

TOP and ABOVE: Concert program and ticket from the 1980 European tour.

RIGHT: Downbeat Pete poses as man of the people, 1980.

With a sleeve designed and commissioned by Pete's pop art hero Peter Blake—and comprised of individual band portraits by such eminent painters as Tom Phillips, Richard Hamilton, Allen Jones, David Hockney, Clive Barker, Ron Kitaj, Howard Hodgkin, Patrick Caulfield, and Blake himself—*Face Dances* was produced by the Eagles' regular studio helmsman, Bill Szymczyk, in the back half of 1980 under a lucrative new deal the band had signed with Warner Bros, which paid them advances of $12 million for three albums. With the exception of John's raucous "The Quiet One," the songs were by Pete and fraught with veiled confessionals, including the bear-pit story, as retold in "Cache Cache." Aside from the dynamic "You Better You Bet," it was an album short on ferocious tension and air-punching, euphoric release, but very long on the contents of Pete's private diary. Yet such was the loyalty of the Who's fan base that it still sold over a million copies in the United States, and did well elsewhere, too.

THE WHO 1981

The Who

TOP: 1981 tour poster.

ABOVE: The single "You Better You Bet."

LEFT: The sleeve of the album *Face Dances* is a showcase for heavyweight British artists.

Slipping out of Control

Behind the scenes, Pete was not the only one with problems. It was a bad time for the Who, the mood overshadowed by the death in London in April 1981 of Kit Lambert, aged forty-five, after a fall following a night of heavy drinking and possibly having been beaten up at a gay club. Roger's younger sister Carol succumbed not long afterward to cancer, aged thirty-two. Like Pete's, John and Kenney's marriages were failing, plus Roger had fallen out with Kenney and, at a band meeting at the time of the release of *Face Dances*, maintained that the lack of explosive drumming meant the album lacked fire. In turn, Kenney blamed Pete's songs, claiming the band's main writer had kept back the best of his recent output for his first solo album proper, *Empty Glass*, released the previous year to acclaim and respectable sales. He had a point, though *Empty Glass* had

TOP: For all their bonhomie, Roger resented how Pete prioritized his solo music over the group's.

ABOVE: Pete's solo album *Empty Glass*.

been recorded over two years in downtime from the Who, with the title track having been recorded by the band but then rejected for *Who Are You*, while the minor hit single, "Rough Boys," which toyed with the idea of bisexuality, felt too personal for Pete to be confident that Roger would sing it without wanting to make big changes.

It was all a mess, yet it was the least committed member of the band, Pete, who called them back together again—feeling that only by recommitting to the Who might he find fresh focus for a life that by the end of 1981 was slipping way out of control in addictions to alcohol, the sedative Ativan and sleeping pills, and now freebase cocaine mixed with heroin. Reuniting with Karen after two years apart, Pete followed in the footsteps of his friend Eric Clapton in seeking treatment from Meg Paterson. Therapy for Pete as well as a contractual obligation, the Who went to work on another album, timed for release before what insiders suspected might be their final, most money-spinning tour.

Back as producer, after Bill Szymczyk was unfairly handed some of the blame for *Face Dances*' deficiencies, was Glyn Johns. All seasoned studio professionals, they cut the album in one month, July 1982, to meet the deadline of a tour booked to start in September. His life a maelstrom in every respect for both good and ill, Pete was keen to draw a line under the album, get the tour done, and retire the Who as a live act, which he felt only put alcoholic and pharmaceutical temptation in his way.

ABOVE: The album *It's Hard*.

LEFT: Roger and Pete working through the Who's 1982 tour.

It's Hard is an album of wordy, extravagantly rhyming songs in a by-now familiar self-absorbed, self-questioning mode (the song "Athena," for example, is about the movie star Theresa Russell, one of a number of women with whom he had fallen in and out of love at this time), and Pete was pleased with his contribution. But, as had been the case with *Empty Glass* before, he was now writing songs for his own solo release as well as songs tailored for the Who and Roger—who hated the album, thinking most of the songs simply not good enough. Though none of them have the irresistibly anthemic or exhilaratingly violent qualities that were the Who's classic trademarks, "Cry if You Want" is a powerful highlight of a solid adult-oriented rock album whose moderate sales, despite the band including several tracks in a live set witnessed by hordes of fans in the stadiums and arenas of North America, seemed to confirm Pete's long-held view that the Who and their fans were now worlds apart: they did not connect to his new work, only wanting a living jukebox of big-hitting oldies.

ABOVE: 1982 concert program and ticket, and the single "Athena."

LEFT: October 13, 1982: the Who at Shea Stadium, New York.

Staggering to the Finish Line

With San Franciscan keyboardist Tim Gorman taking Rabbit's place both on *It's Hard* and on tour, after two warm-up shows in the UK, the Who's three-month trek around the arenas and stadiums of North America took in some vast venues. As a live event, rock was bigger than ever, thanks to a widening audience where members of the Woodstock generation, now in their thirties, were being continually added to by younger fans. Ticketing was now conveniently computerized via credit card payments, parking at the big sports venues was easy, and the growing sophistication of special effects, lighting, and jumbo screens meant that the spectacle could be seen as well as heard however far from the stage. Where in the '70s, big US rock concerts were commonly enjoyed accompanied by weed, wine, and Quaaludes, by the '80s the atmosphere was more often that of a keg party.

At two dates at New York's Shea Stadium, where the Beatles had famously played back in 1965, the Who chose as support act the Clash, a punk band Pete had joined on stage in Brighton, UK, in January 1980 and almost anointed as the Who's successors—their new hit album, *Combat Rock*, having been produced by Glyn Johns. "The Who were very separate people, and I knew them back in the '60s, the days of the High Numbers and Kit Lambert," remembers Clash manager Bernard Rhodes. "At Shea Stadium they had separate limousines, and I said to the Clash, 'Never, ever be like that group; they might be successful but they hate each other; never be like those people—you're different.'" Clash bassist Paul Simonon recalled, "During the Shea Stadium gig and other dates of that tour there was Daltrey and all these miserable gits sitting around who wouldn't talk to us, so Pete Townshend would come into our dressing room and we'd have a game of football."

As it transpired, the Clash would fail to stick together long enough to become the new Who. As for the originals, despite their enormous success as a concert attraction, it was clearly the end of the road. In May 1983, Pete told Roger he would never again tour with the Who, as confirmed in a band meeting a month later, though he did not rule out charity one-offs or special projects. But he was willing to make new Who records. John, however, objected—as far as he was concerned, one without the other would not work. Pete would record but not tour, while John would not record without touring—it was a stalemate. Without fanfare, the news that the Who were, in effect, no more was made public. By way of confirmation, a live album from the '82 tour was released in 1984. Titled *Who's Last*, it made its point over four sides of listless vinyl. Finally, the Who had run out of steam.

ABOVE: The live album *Who's Last*.

OPPOSITE: October 13, 1982, at Shea Stadium, New York: an intimate moment between snappy dressers as the Who quietly call it quits.

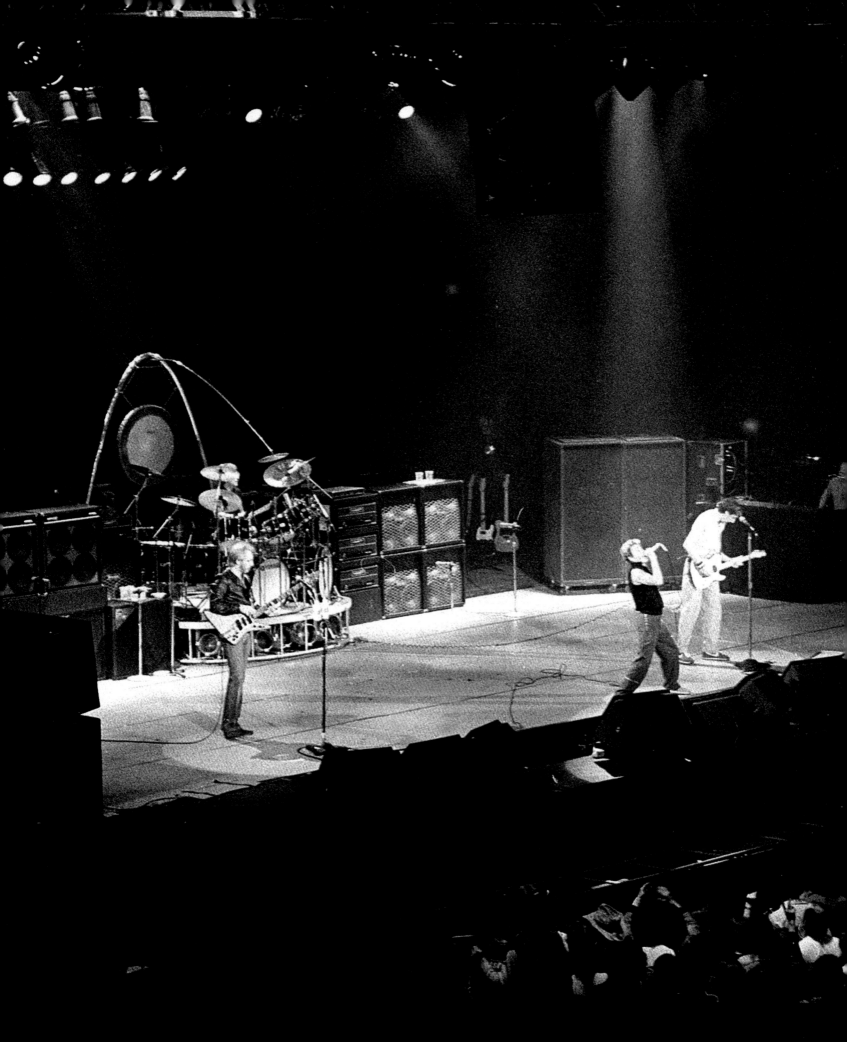

chapter 16

Off...
and On

THE '80S WERE NOT KIND to the rock stars of the '60s. Digital recording and the march of the synthesizer wearied musicians bred on guitars and analog tape; MTV stressed the importance of a pop star's physical attraction to promote records just as the Woodstock generation was wrinkling into their forties; and drink, drugs, and disillusion offered scant defenses against a hungry young generation of musicians eager to supplant the old.

As long as the Who existed, solo side-projects tended to prosper. But with the Who finished, the stock of each member fell, too. Pete's success with

Empty Glass in 1980 had been matched that year by Roger's as star of the Who-produced biopic *McVicar*, about a London armed robber and serial jail-breaker who educated himself behind bars. But of Roger's three subsequent '80s solo albums, only one was not an outright flop. Yet his belief in the Who's integrity as something more than a brand name was unwavering. "I've been saying to Roger for years, 'If you want to go out on tour as the Who, go on!'" Pete told the author in 1989. "'You could be a millionaire, making more money going out than you've ever made in your life.' But he's very religious about it: 'Oh no, it wouldn't be the same, Pete.'"

LEFT: The Who performing on their 1982 tour, the first of their "final" tours.
INSET: *McVicar*, the soundtrack album.

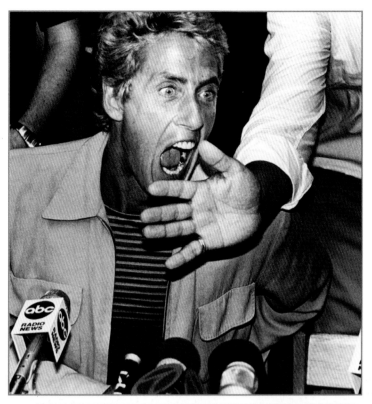

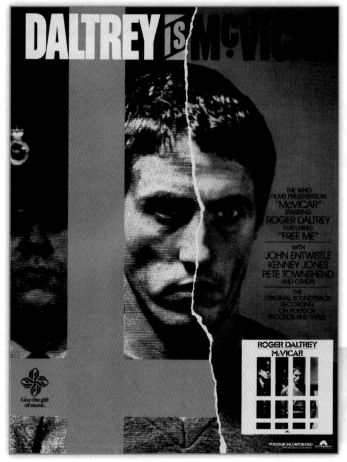

TOP LEFT: Roger goes ballistic at a press conference.

TOP RIGHT: Pete enjoys a crafty puff as Art Garfunkel bends his ear.

ABOVE: Troubled by his hearing, Pete practices backstage on his acoustic guitar, 1986.

LEFT: Roger as McVicar in 1980; thereafter, his screen stardom waned.

Always keener than Roger to make an artistic statement rather than just do a job, Pete's work demanded that you at least heard it. Even so, though his tireless work ethic had him diversifying into publishing as well as making music, his record-buying audience was shrinking.

As good as his word that only a special charity event might convince him to reunite with the Who on stage, Pete reluctantly joined Roger, John, Kenney, and Rabbit onstage at Wembley Stadium, London, on July 13, 1985, for the massive *Live Aid* global telethon benefit for famine relief in Africa, organized by the persuasive Bob Geldof. Creaking ring-rustily through four songs, the Who were no disgrace but the day belonged to Queen, George Michael, and U2.

Three years later, the same lineup of the Who played another short set for a one-off charity show, at London's Royal Albert Hall, this time for the annual televised British Phonographic Industry awards show. The door was creaking open.

BELOW: Pete hangs out at an awards ceremony with Michael Jackson, British pop singer Kim Wilde, and Paul McCartney, 1983.

ABOVE: Taking the applause for *Tommy*'s 20th anniversary performance in 1989; Roger, John, and Pete are joined by, from left, Steve Winwood, Billy Idol, Patti LaBelle, Elton John, and Phil Collins.

BELOW LEFT and RIGHT: John, Roger, and Pete at Live Aid, July 13, 1985.

The Musical by Pete Townshend

Chiefly what had changed was that Pete, having cleaned up his act, had reunited with Karen and hoped to have another child to cement things. Then there was the anxiety of seeing his record sales slide while he was spending large amounts on a very ambitious all-star musical adaptation he was writing and producing of the children's fantasy novel *The Iron Man* by the UK's poet laureate, Ted Hughes, whom Pete had befriended though his work in book publishing.

Manager Bill Curbishley was charged with finding out how much a Who reunion tour might be worth. With old ally Frank Barsalona still at the forefront of the live rock music business in the United States, the sums being quoted as potential earnings were tremendous, especially now that commercial sponsorship could be added to the balance sheet, too.

Would a new Who album help? On the contrary: playing the hits, the favorites, the proven winners was the way to go. And with all that money, the Who could fatten their sound with extra musicians and singers, thus sparing Pete's tinnitus from the worst that their massive amplification as a four-piece had done in the past.

ABOVE: Pete's album *The Iron Man*.

RIGHT: Pete with the Iron Man at its London staging in 1993.

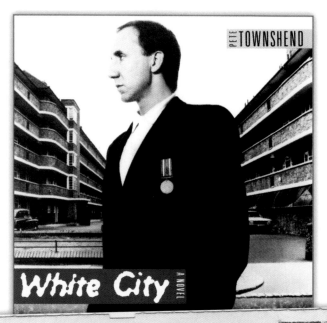

RVEY GOLDSMITH ENTS presents

THE WHO

THE KIDS ARE ALRIGHT TOUR

PM FRI 6 OCT 89

LOCK G H 14

DOORS OPEN 6.00PM LLOYD

AGNT 6-JUL-89

ARENA

National Exhibition Centre
Box Office: Birmingham B40 1NT 021-780 4133
Tickets are purchased subject to the terms and conditions printed overleaf.

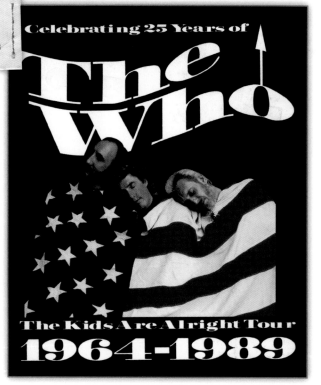

Pete was sold. And, as ever, he found a way of rationalizing his decision, as he told the author at the time, with cheerful cynicism:

"My previous solo album, *White City*, sold about 5,000 copies in the UK, compared to *Empty Glass*, made while the Who was still active, which sold about 220,000; it was a significant jump in the wrong direction. At that time I thought, hell, what would it be like to be forced back to working with the Who by financial starvation, like Brian Poole has to play with the Tremeloes or Gerry has to play with the Pacemakers at the Batley Variety Club? What would it be like? I would die first—and then do it.

"And what's interesting is that I think I have died first. The Who can only do it now because they're absolutely and completely dead. We've got no new product, and we are creatively, clinically dead, so it's just about history. It feels comfortable for people of our age to say we had a great time then and some good stuff came out of it; if you want to hear it, we'll give it to you. In a rather sad way we're behaving like country artists, like a roadshow.

"I don't know whether I'm saying something good or bad about the American rock 'n' roll audience: they're not interested in Robert Plant, Roger Daltrey, Dave Gilmour, Roger Waters, or Pete Townshend—they're interested in Led Zeppelin, the Who, the Stones, the Beatles . . . these institutions that they have created! They're not interested in what they're really all about, but what they represent.

ABOVE: Pete with a pinball machine promoting the hit stage musical version of *Tommy*.

OPPOSITE (clockwise from top left): Pete's album *White City*; 1989 London tour program; 1989 US tour program; compilation album *Who's Better, Who's Best*; and 1989 UK tour ticket.

ABOVE: The remaining three original members in 1990.

OPPOSITE: Pete feeling optimistic about the band and touring, 1990.

"Imagine the scenario: if Led Zeppelin were going out, and it said at the top of the advert that, sadly, Jimmy Page had died, but he will nonetheless be displayed in his coffin in front of the stage, it would not reduce sales by one ticket!

"That's their initial response, but I'm hoping that when they get closer that they'll perhaps change that view."

The Big Band!

With Pete no longer burdened by the angst and personal problems of seven years before, the energy level lacking in the early '80s was fully restored, thanks to a big band there to help out with the musical heavy lifting. With Kenney out and Pete's trusted solo drummer (Simon Philips) and percussionist (Jody Linscott) doing Keith's old job, Rabbit was back on keyboards, and the sound was further fattened by five brass players, three backing singers, and a second guitarist, Steve "Boltz" Bolton. Likewise on a high were the band's traditional stamina (some shows lasted three hours, including solo songs, covers, and such unexpected whimsy as 1967's "Mary Anne with the Shaky Hand") and sense of fun. As Pete told the author, "I suppose what made me want to go with the Who was that I'd got a few royalty statements, and you go down the list and there's 'I'm a Boy' or the mini-opera of the 'Overture' from *Tommy* or 'Cobwebs and Strange' or 'Trick of the Light'—leftfield songs where we showed another side to the *Live at Leeds* archetypical hard-rock side—they're just tuppence, four-pence . . . and then 'Won't Get Fooled Again'—£26,000!

"I thought, hold on a minute, 'Won't Get Fooled Again' comes from a very cynical, apolitical, callous, disdainful part of me, yet the truly generous songs, the songs closest to where I feel my craft really belongs, which is as a disciple of Ray Davies, are unrecognized and forgotten."

Though on that tour the Who never failed to perform "Won't Get Fooled Again," it was the left-field songs that made the shows more than just a money-making exercise but a labor of love.

Not just the Who's 25th anniversary (counting from when Keith joined), it was also *Tommy*'s 20th, and at shows in New York and Los Angeles they performed the opera in full, with cameos by Elton John, Steve Winwood, Phil Collins, Patti LaBelle, and Billy Idol. For Pete, this was a personal highlight, his euphoria heightened by Karen telling him they were expecting a boy, a little brother to their two almost-grown daughters. For Roger, though at age forty-five he needed a yoga instructor to keep him limber and energetic for such a marathon show; the tour was not only where he came most alive but also paid out very handsomely to a man who never lost sight of the bottom line. For John, too—a man with expensive hobbies— the income came in handy.

To crown this lucrative tour around their quarter-century history, on January 17, 1990, the three members of the Who were honored at the Fifth Annual Rock & Roll Hall of Fame induction ceremony, held in the Waldorf Astoria, New York City. They would not reunite again for another six years.

LEFT: Phil Collins in a 1989 performance of *Tommy*.

OPPOSITE: Pete, an inductee, along with the rest of the members of the Who, at the Fifth Annual Rock & Roll Hall of Fame induction ceremony.

Tommy Sets the Stage

While the Who were hibernating, *Tommy* was not. One of many projects into which Pete threw himself—finally at the cost of his marriage to Karen, despite the birth of their son Joseph in 1990—was a stage musical version with the director Des McAnuff. Opening successfully in California in 1992, it transferred in 1993 to Broadway, where it ran for two years, winning five Tony Awards in the process. A production toured Canada in 1995, and a revival played for a year in London's West End beginning in March 1996.

Tommy was making money, but the earnings split as enshrined in the "Tommy Grand Right Document" became the object of a May 1994 claim by Roger and John that they were entitled to more, with the original album, though chiefly Pete's baby, having received plenty of the other band members' creative input along the way. This was of critical importance to the singer and bassist because they earned so much less than songwriter Pete yet had homes, families, and rock-star lifestyles to maintain. Having lived the life of a country squire since the '70s, Roger even had a trout fishery, yet that was nothing compared to John's extravagance. At Quarwood, his fifty-five-room, forty-two-acre estate at Stow-on-the-Wold, Gloucestershire, he collected—despite never learning to drive—Cadillacs, Thunderbirds, and a Rolls-Royce converted into a station wagon to accommodate his Irish wolfhound, Fits Perfectly. And then there were the teapots, toys, suits of armor,

ABOVE: No longer in the Who, Kenney devoted himself to playing polo.

BELOW: Roger at the 7th Annual New York Music Awards at the Beacon Theater, New York, on October 10, 1992.

OPPOSITE: The *Thirty Years of Maximum R&B* CD boxed set.

weaponry (especially Wild West guns), train sets, lighters, Disney and Marilyn Monroe porcelain, guitars and basses, rugs, fine art, photography, skeletons, vintage brandies, wines, and Cuban cigars. Missing Keith every day, John thus kept his zany, excessive, and ruinously expensive spirit alive.

Even as their lawyers were at war over this simmering issue, it did not prevent Roger deciding to celebrate his fiftieth birthday in early '94 with *A Celebration: The Music of Pete Townshend and the Who* (a.k.a. *Daltrey Sings Townshend*), which broke box-office records over two nights at New York's Carnegie Hall and spun off a live album and commercial video. With the Who's music arranged for orchestra by Michael Kamen, guests included John Entwistle, Eddie Vedder, Sinéad O'Connor, Lou Reed, David Sanborn, Alice Cooper, Linda Perry, the Chieftains—and, despite his feeling his usual cold feet about reconstituting the Who, Pete Townshend.

The show then went on tour, minus Pete but with his brother Simon on guitar, and, on drums, Ringo's son Zak Starkey. Born in 1965, Zak had been a Who fan since finding *Meaty, Beaty, Big, and Bouncy* in his parent's record collection, and was doubly enthralled because, as Ringo told the author, "Keith and I were friends. He is 'Uncle Keith' to my children." More than just an uncle, Keith became Zak's role model as a drummer.

Zak's playing style and childhood connection to Keith would help rekindle the Who's musical chemistry. And, with collaborators Ken Russell and Des McAnuff having now seen *Tommy*'s full operatic narrative successfully screened and staged, Pete's thoughts turned to his other great work, *Quadrophenia*.

Quad: The Musical

"The thread that connects *Tommy* and *Quadrophenia*," Pete told the author, "is that they're all about childhood. I've always felt like I was in a unique position in being able to make this claim for the whole of rock 'n' roll as well—if it suits me. All good rock 'n' roll is music that appeals to the essence of the human soul, which is not the baby or the adolescent inside you but the child.

"If there's any kind of interesting struggle that goes on in adolescence—when we start to wear blue jeans, try and drink too much beer, smoke cigarettes, and learn how to stand properly on the street corner—what we're trying to deal with then is what we want to try and drag from childhood into adulthood.

"For some people, adolescence is very brief and for others it goes on forever. For a lot of people in the modern world, adolescence is a long, drawn-out thing. I was still suffering from or enjoying adolescence when I was about twenty-six, maybe even thirty. And I think I've only just recently finished that job, and the last little bit of work is almost like a psychotherapeutic or psychoneurotic process. It's when you finally say that you just can't spend the whole of your life when you're eighty worrying about how you felt when you were six years old, worrying about your relationship with your mother, wondering why your father, the greatest protective figure in your life, wasn't more—or less—disciplinarian.

"All those things you have to stop worrying about yet they seem to me to be at the heart of what you might call 'great rock.' The great definitive rock songs talk to the child bit of me."

Pete could see another thread connecting the two operas, too. "At the end of *Tommy* and *Quadrophenia*, there's death. I just don't view death in the psychoneurotic way that most people do. I look upon death as being redemption."

Such were the teachings of Meher Baba. But Pete was also signaling what actually happened to Jimmy at the end of *Quadrophenia*, which back in 1973 had been ambiguous. Now the story had a clear conclusion.

Bringing *Quadrophenia* to the stage was an ambition Pete had felt would not be realized because of the cost, the mod opera never having had the mass appeal of *Tommy* in the vital U.S. market. But in early 1996, Des McAnuff suggested that a performance to celebrate August's 50th anniversary of the Vespa scooter could be financed by the Italian manufacturer, Piaggio. Then the Prince's Trust, a charity founded by Prince Charles to help young people, entered the scene, bringing with it sponsorship from MasterCard, which would underwrite the production costs of a show to take place that summer in London's Hyde Park.

To pull the crowds, though, it needed the Who. Pete found himself in the rare position of begging Roger, who did not fancy being bossed around by the creative genius, especially as he was in dispute with him over the *Tommy* money. Having been reassured that, since working with

McAnuff, Pete now understood the meaning of the word "collaboration," Roger agreed, and the pair worked on the script. John could never resist live performance, and Zak completed the basic band for what, Pete stressed, was not a 'Who concert' but 'a Who thing,' the first ever live performance of *Quadrophenia* in its entirety, with parts being played by special guests, to take place on June 29, 1996, during a day-long bill that included Eric Clapton, Bob Dylan, and Alanis Morissette. All 150,000 tickets sold in forty-eight hours.

The cast included the *Quadrophenia* movie's star Phil Daniels as narrator, glam-rocker Gary Glitter (who shortly afterward was exposed as a pedophile and is currently serving a sixteen-year prison sentence in the UK for child sex offenses) as the Godfather, comedian Adrian Edmondson as Ace Face/Bellboy, actor Stephen Fry as the hotel guest, and Trevor McDonald as the news reader. Additional musicians included Simon Townshend, Rabbit, and Pink Floyd's David Gilmour. Despite Roger appearing in an eye patch (having been struck in the eye by a mic stand swung by Gary

Glitter during rehearsals), Pete's voice being out of condition, the sound mix being problematic, and the day being cold, the event was a success. Minus Gilmour but plus Billy Idol, the production crossed the Atlantic for six nights at New York's Madison Square Garden, where fans were also treated to the Who classics "Behind Blue Eyes," "Won't Get Fooled Again," "Magic Bus," "Naked Eye," and "Substitute."

Clearly getting on and enjoying themselves, the Who hit the road with a revised *Quadrophenia*, touring North America before returning to the UK and then, in spring '97, Europe (with P. J. Proby taking over from Gary Glitter), and then back to the United States for the summer, winding up in Palm Beach, Florida, on August 16.

Zak had transformed the band. No longer would Pete have to contort himself into just the occasional reunion. Growing older, the Who now seemed hungry to live again.

ABOVE and BELOW: 1997 *Quadrophenia* tour ticket and poster.

OPPOSITE: 1997 *Quadrophenia* tour program.

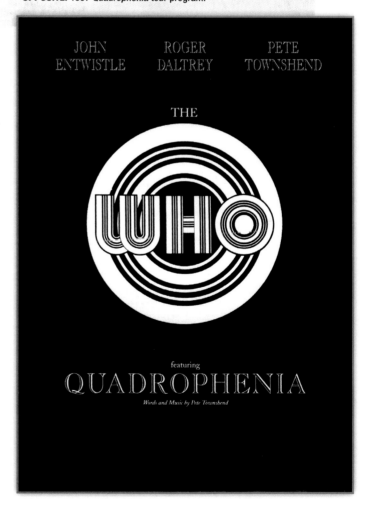

chapter 17

And Then There Were Two

BACK IN 1971'S *LIFEHOUSE,* Pete had predicted the emergence of the Internet and virtual reality, and by the late '90s these were not just futuristic concepts but an entirely new means of communicating and living that was happening for real. Pete remained fascinated by new technology and how it shapes us humans. Buoyed by how the 1996 and 1997 tours had rehabilitated *Quadrophenia*, he now felt it was *Lifehouse*'s turn to get more of an airing on-stage, though he would not try to reconstitute in its entirety a work he admitted had never been finished.

LEFT: John playing one of his bespoke basses with the Ringo Starr band, 1995.

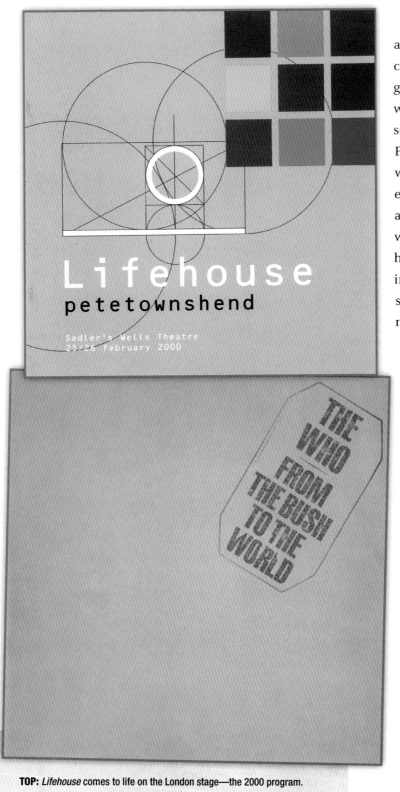

Lifehouse
petetownshend

Sadler's Wells Theatre
25/26 February 2000

THE WHO FROM THE BUSH TO THE WORLD

TOP: *Lifehouse* comes to life on the London stage—the 2000 program.

ABOVE: Based on the *Live at Leeds* album sleeve, the 2000 tour program.

OPPOSITE: Concert ticket from the 2000 tour.

Pete was also energized not only by the Keith-alike drumming of Zak Starkey but also by rediscovering his pleasure in playing full-tilt electric guitar, having played mostly acoustic in 1989. But what prompted a return to the road in 1999 so soon after getting off it in 1997 was an appeal to Pete and Roger by their manager Bill Curbishley, who told them that John, a compulsive collector of expensive items, had got into financial difficulties, and now the bank was bouncing his checks. There was never any doubt that his old friends would help the bassist make a living, though Pete groused in private that he was endangering his hearing just so John—who needed two hearing aids himself, now—didn't have to move to a smaller house.

"The relationship between Roger, John, and I is the same relationship as when I first met Roger Daltrey on the stairs of Acton County Grammar School. He was in the year above me, a lout with a guitar—I was thirteen and John and I already had a group," Pete had recalled to the author. "There were three groups in school and we were just one of them. Three little snotty-nosed school kids with mashed potato on our lapels! When we gather together today, that's what we feel. Nothing has changed."

So, tentatively, the Who reunited in 1999 to play a mix of charity benefits and paying gigs. And though the decision may well have been determined by the desire to reduce overheads and make these shows as profitable as possible, for the first time in nearly twenty years, the Who played stripped back down to a five-piece, with Rabbit on keyboards.

Dressed in a crewneck shirt, his hair cut short, Roger had something of the 1964 mod look. And though Pete's graying locks had long retreated from a shiny forehead, his button-down shirt, suit, and shades also evoked nights at the

Railway Hotel. Save for a few acoustic excursions on his Gibson J-200, Pete had returned full-time to a Fender Stratocaster for the first time since 1968, playing with a fluidity and windmilling ferocity that belied his years and fatherhood of a daughter now aged thirty. Always his own man, the bearded silver fox John displayed new heights of bass virtuosity—on spectacular display on a long solo during the *Quadrophenia* hit "5.15"—with a look likewise rooted in the mid-1970s. Creaking only a little despite both now being in their mid-fifties, Roger and Peter clearly had a rapport, and the shows rocked harder and more excitingly than any since Keith was still alive.

Part of the reason they were so vibrant was that they were scheduled as one-offs or in short clusters rather than in the long, draining treks of a full-blown tour. After just seven gigs in 1999, the following year the Who played thirty-eight shows in four legs, three in the United States and one in Europe, each leg seldom exceeding a fortnight on the road. At London's Royal Albert Hall on November 27, the tour ended at a benefit show that raised £1 million (around $1.6 million) for the Teenage Cancer Trust, a cause dear to the hearts of the entire band. In this three-and-a-half-hour show the classical violinist Nigel Kennedy played the outro on what may well have been the definitive live performance of "Baba O'Riley," and other guests included Who fanatics Bryan Adams, Eddie Vedder of Pearl Jam, Paul Weller (formerly of the Jam), and Noel Gallagher of Oasis.

On October 20, 2001, at Madison Square Garden at the all-star tribute to the victims of the 9/11 terrorist attack, the Who, more than any other act, captured the passion and defiance of the fans and the moment as they performed "Who Are You," "Baba O'Riley," "Behind Blue Eyes," and "Won't Get Fooled Again."

It was a special performance, and those same energy levels continued into the following year as the Who played five dates in the UK before pausing ahead of three months of summer dates in North America. Rehearsing for the tour, Pete and Roger had grown a little concerned that the somewhat overweight John was hitting the Remy Martin brandy early in the day and had spells of edgy chattiness. But so great was his playing, as ever, that they put their concerns to one side.

Then, at 3:00 a.m. on June 27, 2002, on the eve of the first night of the North American tour in Las Vegas, John retired to his room at the Hard Rock Hotel and Casino with a groupie named Alycen Rowse. The following morning she awoke at 10:00 a.m. to find John dead. Aged fifty-seven, he still smoked, had a blocked artery as well as hypertension, and, the medical examiner determined, cocaine had contributed to the heart attack that killed him.

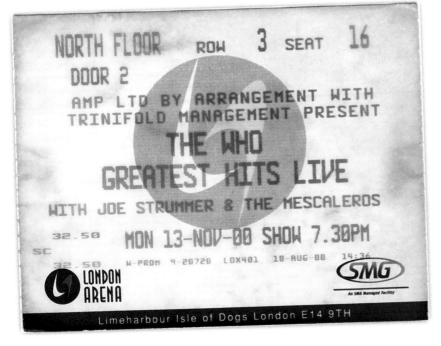

The news came as a terrible shock to his old bandmates, who had known John since school, some forty-six years before. Bu they had an immediate decision to make: to cancel or find a way to carry on. Given the suspicion—correct, as it proved—that cocaine had played a part in his death, there was no guarantee that the insurers would pay out to cover the road crew and other costs if the Who canceled. They spoke to John's son Christopher, who assured Pete and Roger they should carry on if possible. The Welsh virtuoso jazz-influenced bassist Pino Palladino, who had played on Pete's solo work, was contacted in Philadelphia as he was about to fly home to the UK; instead he flew west and rehearsed intensively for a first show that would now fall on July 1 at the Hollywood Bowl. It would be an intensely emotional performance.

After three more gigs, Pete and Roger flew home to say goodbye to their old friend. On July 10 at St. Edwards, a tiny twelfth-century church opposite Quarwood, John's funeral proved as rock 'n' roll as his life and death, with the vicar running off with John's girlfriend, Lisa Pritchett-Johnson (who fatally overdosed three years later). Almost the biggest shock came when it was revealed that John, the former tax office clerk turned rock 'n' roll hellraiser, had for decades been a secret Freemason.

The 2002 tour ended, as was traditional, in Toronto. With John's death, his share of the proceeds had gone to Roger and Pete, who despite this was in no mood to return to the fray any time soon. Pete's lack of enthusiasm irritated Roger, but a year later, Roger would be there for Pete as he faced the greatest crisis of his life.

The Dark Net

Charity was central to the teachings of Meher Baba,

so when, in 1998, Pete was moved by a documentary recording the plight of children in Russian orphanages, his impulse was to help by making a donation. So he keyed "russian orphanages boys donations" into his browser search engine—and was horrified as, on his screen, images of children being abused appeared. The trauma of what happened with his grandmother Denny came flooding back, and Pete was profoundly shaken. The memories had always been there, shaping his songs of childhood abuse and sexual exploitation, from "I'm a Boy" and "A Quick One, While He's Away" to *Tommy*, for which Pete could not bear to write the most explicit songs, "Cousin Kevin" and "Fiddle About," so had given them to John to write.

Rather than putting the lid back on these memories, Pete decided to do something about it by helping other victims. Aside from funding counseling for victims of abuse, he also decided he would use his platform as a rock star with a popular website to publicize the link between child abuse, online pedophile pornography, and its financial beneficiaries, including Internet service providers and the financial institutions that handled online payments. He wanted to prove that a bank would take your money to access child porn online, so, logging what he was doing, and keeping a colleague in the United States informed, he paid seven dollars on his Barclaycard to access such a site. Having landed on the home page, he went no further but canceled the payment, satisfied that he had achieved what he set out to prove.

What he did not know was the FBI had logged his access and payment, and passed on details to the British police, whose Operation Ore was collating evidence to prosecute those who accessed online child porn. Such was the cozy relationship between the police in Britain and certain media outlets that Pete's name was leaked to a national newspaper, which on January 11, 2003, ran a front-page story on an unnamed millionaire rock guitarist under investigation.

Knowing at once that the newspaper meant him, Pete released a statement to tell his side of the story and handed himself in at his local police station. In their interview, the police indicated that they believed his account to be true, but that by accessing the website he had broken the law, and his profile and consequent media attention meant the matter could not be allowed to drop. Pete's home and studio was searched and eleven computers taken away for analysis. Meanwhile, Pete's friends, including Mick Jagger and David Bowie, sent messages of support. But it was Roger who laid his reputation on the line with a determination and passion that most touched Pete.

Over the next four months, Pete waited while the police analyzed his computers and waited for any accusers to come forward, but on both counts Pete was clean. In May, Pete was given a choice of either going to trial or accepting a formal police caution and having his name entered at the lowest level of the sex offenders register. Worn out, Pete chose the latter, but later regretted that he had not chosen the bolder course to clear his name entirely. Even so, public opinion ran largely in his favor, and Roger's credibility as a tough, working-class, no-nonsense guy did a lot to persuade those more hard-nosed people, for whom child abuse was so beyond the pale as to taint anyone it touched, that Pete was not a pedophile after all, and that his story,

complicated and strange though it was, was true.

Roger's unstinting support throughout this crisis moved Pete to gratitude and full appreciation of everything he had done for him over the years, though they remained chalk and cheese. Besides, they were now pushing sixty, and since John's death they were the only ones left. Pete decided to rededicate himself to the thing that Roger loved most: his baby, his band, the Who.

ABOVE: The 2002 tour program.

chapter 18

The Who Reborn

BACK IN 1989, the band had recorded a song called "Dig" for Pete's solo adaptation of Ted Hughes' children's book *The Iron Man*. Now they were back in the studio to record a pair of songs to be released as a single and to give the planned hits compilation album *Then and Now* some up-to-date content. If Pete owed Roger, Roger owed the guy who inspired him in the first place as an angry Acton schoolboy to rebel and rock: Elvis. Quoting musically and lyrically from the King's 1961 hit "Can't Help Falling in Love," Pete wrote a song that contrasted the "Real Good Looking Boy" of the song's title with his ugly misfit mate, his lack of handsomeness pointed out to him—in a half echo of "I'm a Boy"—by his own mother.

LEFT: Performing live on November 13, 2000.

The single's second track, "Old Red Wine," moves from maudlin to defiant. The band had tried to record it while John was alive, but now that he was gone, was dedicated to the fallen comrade. With Zak, Rabbit, and Pete's brother Simon on board, the songs were arguably better than anything by the band since *Who Are You*. And the star was Roger: though his voice was losing range with age, it was growing in subtlety and compelling character. As the Oscar-winning soundtrack composer and veteran songwriter Randy Newman told the author, "I always thought that Daltrey was lucky to be in that band twirling the mic round, but no, he isn't. I was listening to one of their very early records, with 'Substitute.' It was this very corrosively cynical, satirical stuff, and Daltrey was adding to it by the nature of his vocals. He gets it—he really gets it. He helps those songs. They were an unbelievably good rock band, as good as they ever got."

Buoyed by how well these new songs turned out, Pete was now ready to take it further: a whole new album.

Back in 1993, Pete had released a solo album titled *Psychoderelict*, a musical drama that combined some of the elements of *Lifehouse*—the project whose lack of resolution continued to nag at its creator—with some fresh ideas. Ray High from *Lifehouse* was now a gloomy projection of Pete himself, a reclusive rock star who gets caught up in the tabloid world of deceit and—in an eerily prophetic moment—a scandal involving underage sexual obsession.

Long on self-absorption, clunky narrative, and character, but short on memorable songs, *Psychoderelict* had flopped. Pete retreated from presenting his Big Ideas so publicly, though he fell in love with the Internet as a means by which to communicate directly to fans without the media. He was also developing a new work, *The Boy Who Heard Music*, a novella and an opera plot that moved on the story of *Psychoderelict*'s Ray to where he was now a background character in a narrative that reprises many elements from *Lifehouse*, chiefly the idea of the Grid (foreshadowing the Internet), and, from *Tommy*, the concept of a mirror being smashed or passed through.

LEFT (from top): The *Then and Now* compilation album; the single "Real Good Looking Boy"; and Pete's 1993 album, *Psychoderelict*.

OPPOSITE: Backstage at Madison Square Garden with Rolling Stones' Keith Richards at the 9/11 benefit concert for New York City on October 20, 2001.

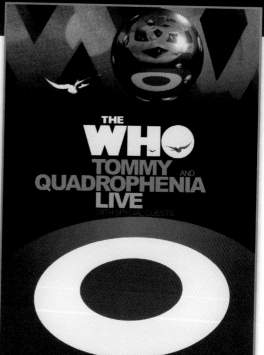

TOP: Still the birdman forty years on: Pete performs in Australia on July 28, 2004.

ABOVE (from left): The *Wire & Glass* EP; the *Endless Wire* album; and the *Tommy and Quadrophenia Live* DVD.

What was new was a dramatization of a friendship between a Christian, a Muslim, and a Jew, and there was no shortage of symbolism and significance if one took the trouble to work out exactly what Pete was driving at. But where back in 1971 Pete had thrown himself into presenting *Lifehouse* in all its complexity and purity before being ground down by time pressures and practicalities, in 2005 he decided to cut to the chase and, without further ado, embrace the benefit his work received when heard under the popular banner of the Who rather than ignored as yet another Pete project no one could get their heads around.

Retitled *Wire & Glass*, this work-in-progress mini-opera would form one-half of a new album that took its title, *Endless Wire*, from a song prompted by Roger's practical response back in 1971 to Pete's *Lifehouse* concept of the Grid: to connect everybody, there wasn't enough wire in the world. Recorded and mostly played in his own studios as if a Pete solo album but with Roger singing most songs and instrumental contributions from Rabbit, Zak, Pino, and Simon, *Endless Wire* took its time to reach fruition, finally being released in October 2006, four months after the tour set up to promote it.

Though the album was late, it was worth waiting for. If *Who's Next* was the brilliant compromise between *Lifehouse*'s vision of purity and life's gritty expediency, then *Endless Wire* was a *Who's Next* for the new millennium. As much was signaled by the opening synth ripple, echoing "Baba O'Riley," of the new album's first track, "Fragments," the product of a collaboration with composer Lawrence Ball to make real 1971's concept of music created based on the input of an individual listener. Though part of the *Boy Who Heard Music* concept, in a typically confusing Pete gambit this song did not fit into the *Wire & Glass* mini-opera that occupied the album's second half. Nor was *Wire & Glass* clear as a story, but the music was excellent, a highlight being Pete's tribute to his musical aunt in "Trilby's Piano," beautifully orchestrated by Rachel Fuller, who had come to occupy the role of Pete's permanent partner after the final collapse of his marriage to Karen and numerous love affairs. Pete would pay tribute to her in the album's most poignant song, "You Stand by Me." As he explained at the time, "It is for her, and for Roger, for believing in me, and standing by me when I have been completely out of order. It could be for many of my family, friends, and fans who have done the same. I have often been a very tricky man to live with."

ABOVE: Pete still rocking in 2006 on tour in Germany.

As ever, movies and other music were big inspirations to Pete, with Mel Gibson's *The Passion of the Christ* prompting both "Two Thousand Years" and "A Man in a Purple Dress," while "It's Not Enough" came to him after he saw Jean-Luc Godard's classic *Le Mépris* starring Brigitte Bardot. More idiosyncratically still, Pete paid tribute to the country legend in "God Speaks of Marty Robbins" while "Mike Post Theme" honored the man who made the music for *Law & Order*, *The A-Team*, *NYPD Blue*, *The Rockford Files*, *L.A. Law*, *Quantum Leap*, *Magnum, P.I.*, and *Hill Street Blues*.

As punchy as it was idiosyncratic, and very far from the sound of a band going through the motions and recycling old tricks, *Endless Wire* was a success without being a blockbuster, and is one of those albums that rewards each new listen.

The Who had toured lightly in 2004, including a first trip to Japan as well as a first visit to Australia for the first time since 1968's ill-tempered foray, and in July 2005 they played at Live 8 in London's Hyde Park, the benefit concert marking the 20th anniversary of Live Aid. A far longer trek was planned to last from June 2006 to October 2007, covering Europe and North America, and taking in shows as intimate as Leeds University's refectory hall, where they had recorded their legendary 1970 live album, and as vast as the Glastonbury Festival, which they headlined to 170,000 fans. Zak, Pino, Rabbit, and Simon fleshed out the band, allowing Roger and Pete—both now in their sixties—to pace themselves.

But Roger's voice broke down badly on occasion, and in the end he needed surgery to remove

ABOVE: Live in Atlantic City on November 24, 2006.

precancerous throat lesions. The road and the rock 'n' roll lifestyle had taken Keith and John, and in the early '80s it almost claimed Pete, too. But now the ferociously fit and drink- and drug-shunning Roger was succumbing to ordinary wear and tear, the years of never holding back when he had a microphone in his hand taking their toll. The Who were now entering that stage in their career where every tour was a victory lap, unmissable because it may never come 'round again.

TOP LEFT and ABOVE: 2007 tour tickets and the 2006 tour program.

LEFT: Roger and Pete perform at The Who Unplugged Mini-Show and Press Conference at the Berlin Fritz Club in Berlin, Germany, on July 13, 2006.

The Victory Lap

Age slows you down, and over the last eight years the Who—that warring but now mostly reconciled pair of opposites, Roger and Pete—have taken care to prioritize what they want to do and pace themselves doing it.

Charity is important to both men, and shows for the Teenage Cancer Trust and Teen Cancer America Benefit have been at the heart of their live excursions. In the five years from 2008, the Who played 86 shows all over the world. By contrast, in the year 1965 alone, they played over 250 shows. During this long series of victory laps, some of the shows were no more than cameos— for example a six-song acoustic duet of "Let's See

Action," "Behind Blue Eyes," "Two Thousand Years," "Mike Post Theme," "Won't Get Fooled Again," and "Tea and Theatre."

Finally, the pair had conquered the inhibition about getting too intimate, as Pete had revealed to the author years earlier. "Roger wanted to do the Everly Brothers' 'Love Hurts' just with two guitars, and then he said, 'Let's do that song from *Who's Next*, "Too Much of Anything"'—he loves this silly little song. So we started rehearsing it, but it wouldn't gel, so to make it work we had to gaze into one another's eyes like the Everlys. He laughed awkwardly, because our eyes don't often meet in conversation . . ."

At the other end of the cameo scale were the band's full electric appearances at global sporting events, the first being their halftime show for Super Bowl XLIV in Miami's Dolphin Stadium on February 7, 2010. Roger's striped blazer and scarf revived a 1965 mod fashion, echoed by Pete's porkpie hat and shades, though his untucked shirt would never have passed muster down the old Scene Club. Pulling out all the slam-bang lightshow, laser, pyrotechnical, and windmilling stops (despite Pete's having a problem shoulder to add to the return of tinnitus), they played a medley of "Pinball Wizard," "Baba O'Riley"—in which Roger teasingly sang the line "Let's get together before we get much older" while gazing straight across the stage at Pete—"Who Are You," "See Me Feel Me," and "Won't Get Fooled Again." Two years later, on August 12, at the closing

ABOVE: 2009 tour program.

LEFT and BELOW: Rocking the Super Bowl XLIV Halftime Show at Sun Life Stadium in Miami Gardens, Florida, on February 7, 2010.

ceremony for the 2012 Olympic Games in London they performed a medley of "Baba O'Riley," "See Me, Feel Me," and "My Generation."

In March 2010, the Who revived *Quadrophenia* at their London Teenage Cancer Trust Concert at London's Royal Albert Hall, Pearl Jam's Eddie Vedder duetting with Daltrey on "The Punk and the Godfather." While *Tommy* had gone out and made its fortune several times over since 1969, *Quadrophenia* had endured a difficult launch and never built the popular momentum of the older work. Now, forty years on from its original birth pangs, the Who decided to take it on the road again, performing it in full with a selection of other favorites as encores.

RIGHT and BELOW: Rocking the Closing Ceremony of the London Olympic Games at Olympic Stadium on August 12, 2012.

OPPOSITE (from top): *Quadrophenia* live album and DVD; 2014 *Quadrophenia* live tour program; and Roger's solo career revives.

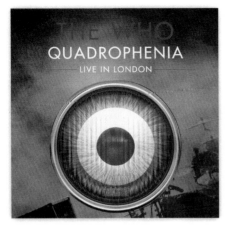

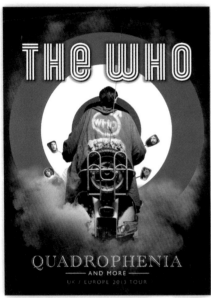

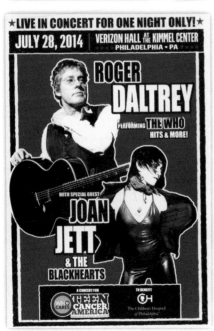

Nor was Pete done with the mod opera; like Lou Reizner's 1972 *Tommy*, it has now been orchestrated by his partner Rachel Fuller for release on the classical Deutsche Grammophon label in summer 2015, with a world premiere concert at the Royal Albert Hall, London on July 5, starring Pete, with Alfie Boe singing Roger's parts, backed by the forces of the Royal Philharmonic Orchestra and the London Oriana Choir.

Roger, too, celebrated the mod era in surprising and extremely successful fashion by teaming up with another guitarist who worshipped the hard rhythmic chop of Mick Green of the pre-Beatles Brit-rockers Johnny Kidd & the Pirates—Wilko Johnson (aka John Wilkinson), who had found fame in the mid-'70s with proto-punk R&B revivalists Dr. Feelgood. Becoming pals after being sat together at an awards ceremony, Roger and Wilko decided to do something about their mutual passion for that style of gritty, bluesy British rock, and what resulted was *Going Back Home*, which sounded as if, in a parallel universe, the High Numbers had stuck at it. Poignantly, by the time Roger was free to record it after coming off the road with the Who, Wilko had been diagnosed with terminal pancreatic cancer and given little time to live. In November 2013, he was well enough for the pair to record eleven tracks in a week, and *Going Back Home* was released the following March, just as Roger turned seventy. Not only was it a big UK hit, making it to No. 3, but a month later, Wilko's condition turned out to be operable after all, and the death sentence was lifted.

Not all their contemporaries were so lucky as the Who celebrated their half-century since Keith joined. In late 2013, Lou Reed, who had been one of their support acts at the first Charlton show in 1974, died six months after a liver transplant. A year later, within three weeks of each other in December 2014, their fellow Woodstock star and regular support act in 1968 and 1969, Joe Cocker, died of lung cancer, and the great keyboard player with fellow bill-sharers the (Small) Faces, Ian McLagan, fell victim to a fatal stroke. He had married Keith's ex-wife Kim a month after the drummer's death, but had lost her to a road accident in 2006. The reminders that nothing and no one last forever were coming thick and fast.

In 2014, the Who announced their 50th anniversary tour—"the beginning of the long goodbye," according to Roger—and recorded a new song to bring up to date their latest singles and hit tracks compilation album, *The Who Hits 50!* "Be Lucky" found lyricist Pete in

TOP LEFT: Wilko Johnson and Roger perform for Pancreatic Cancer UK at the Porchester Hall, London, on March 20, 2014.

TOP RIGHT: Pino Palladino and Wilko Johnson during rehearsals in London for The Who's 50th Anniversary Gig for The Teenage Cancer Trust on November 10, 2014.

ABOVE: Pete and Eddie Vedder during rehearsals in London for The Who's 50th Anniversary Gig for The Teenage Cancer Trust on November 10, 2014.

INSET: Wilko Johnson and Roger's album, *Going Back Home*.

cheery mood, cryptically but catchily name-checking both AC/DC and Daft Punk in a rocking manifesto, which kept its deeper meaning ambiguous and tongue in cheek.

As the Who embark on their long goodbye, perhaps it is only fitting that Pete, who had a lot to say twenty-five years previously when contemplating another anniversary tour, has the last word. He would not wish it any other way.

"On the Who's birthday, it shouldn't slide by. This is my life; I've spent my whole life doing this. Don't I owe it to fans of the band and people who grew up with the music? And if I owe anything, what is it that I owe? I owe it to myself that that material is kept as alive as possible while I'm alive and the anniversary should encourage retrospectives of our work and acknowledgement of it and treatment of it as art. I think I was the first person to claim that rock music was art and I've always believed in it implicitly and passionately. It is living art, as important to me as a good book, the theater, cinema, ballet—and often much more important. It's not pomposity or pretentiousness, it's a statement of fact.

"I also want to show where the Who came from. When we first played in Shepherd's Bush, we only had one song, 'Can't Explain'—maybe not even that. What did we play in those days? James Brown, Howlin' Wolf, Bo Diddley, Ray Charles—I even used to do a few jazz songs, Barney Kessel tunes, which went down amazingly well with the mods of the day. Jazz was part of what we came from; we came from a very broad musical spectrum but we specialized in one area, and now we're responsible for the narrowness of lots of aspects of heavy metal music.

BELOW: Performing at the O2 Arena in London on June 15, 2013.

If you can trace that back to *Live at Leeds*, then maybe we should try and open that door again . . .

"It sounds like a bit of a cause I'm on.

"Rock 'n' roll came from America, it's their fucking music—and they know less about it than we do. In the '60s I went to America and I fucking lectured them. I used to say to people like [*Rolling Stone* editor] Jann Wenner, 'Do you listen to fucking rhythm and blues? Do you know who John Lee Hooker is? Do you really think that rock 'n' roll is Jefferson fucking Airplane?' And they listened, and now it's time to go back and lecture them again.

"I think one of the reasons why American audiences are so enthusiastic to see the band is that they're not sure what the context really is. English music-lovers are much more analytical, more academic. They read more, they talk more, they collect records in a different way. It's very rare you see an English rock fan who attaches themselves exclusively to one artist as the Americans do. I'm familiar with that because I know lots of people who only ever listen to Who albums as far as I can see.

"What they're looking for in America is context,

they want to understand why rock 'n' roll still matters, why it's such a part of American life. It's a part of high commerce—advertisers depend on it, they can't sell half the products they want to without rock 'n' roll music. 'Won't Get Fooled Again' is a necessary part of the commercial institution of America.

"I'd been in the vanguard of modern rock writing since the beginning, and it's been important to me to fight the journalists around me, to have my own view which was as informed and academic and intelligent as theirs—and as objective. I try to look at my work as a journalist would, and try to work out what has been going on. It's been really important to me just to know what it was I was doing.

"But it's very much a *was* in my case—I don't think I'm working in the vanguard anymore, that was only for the first five or six years of the Who. When it stopped, I suddenly felt, why is it I can't do it any more? I then spent the next twenty years trying to work out why. For a long time I thought it was my age, and a lot of people make that mistake with the idea that it has something to do with being

ABOVE: Fifty years on and still rocking hard at the O2 Arena in London, March 22, 2015.

OPPOSITE: The 2014 single "Be Lucky" and compilation album *The Who Hits 50!*

youthful at eighty years old. I've met eighty-year-old ladies and you say to them what is it that makes you sparkle? And they say, 'I feel like a little girl inside.'

"It's only recently that I felt I've discovered what really makes good rock important to me. I loved it so much. The first rhythm and blues I played completely, utterly transformed my life. Discovering rock for me, which was then in the shape of rhythm and blues—Bo Diddley, Jimmy Reed, Chuck Berry, John Lee Hooker, the first heavy rhythmic electric rockers—it was like, 'Eureka!' It was such an incredible moment; I've been trying to find out for years why it was so incredible.

"Then, like somebody who's struck oil and wants to find more, you wonder *why* you have to find more. What is it about the human spirit that makes

you so greedy as to want more and more of the same thing over and over again? What is it about us that means that 'Heard It Through the Grapevine' is not enough? Why do we have to have a new version?

"Why is it that when we wake up in the morning, we hope that when we switch on the radio we'll hear something that will affect the skin on the back of our neck? And hopefully it will be something that we've never heard before but we will recognize as the *spice*, the *stuff*, and we'll say: '*Yeah!* What makes it rock for me is it has to go straight in and make me shudder.' *That's* rock 'n' roll!"

Photography Credits

Unless otherwise noted below, all memorabilia (album covers, posters, ads, etc.) was graciously provided by Christian Suchatzki (www.the-who.net).

CHAPTER 6: BREAKTHROUGH!

pp.40–41: © Rex—David Magnus/REX

p.42: © J. Barry Peake/REX

p.43, bottom: © Pictorial Press Ltd./Alamy

pp.44–45: © Pictorial Press Ltd./Alamy

p.47, top left: Dezo Hoffmann/REX

CHAPTER 7: POP ART STARS!

pp.48–49: © Kay Cooper/REX

pp.50–51: © Ray Stevenson/REX

p.52: © Hugh Vanes/REX

p.54: © Michael Ochs Archives/Getty Images

p.55: © Chris Morphet/Redferns/Getty Images

pp.56–57: © Chris Morphet/Redferns/Getty Images

p.57, top: © Pictorial Press Ltd./Alamy

p.59, top: © Ron Howard/Redferns/Getty Images

p.59, bottom left: © Chris Morphet/Redferns/Getty Images

p.59, bottom right: © Chris Morphet/Redferns/Getty Images

pp.60–61: © Ivan Keeman/Redferns/Getty Images

CHAPTER 8: FAR OUT!

pp.62–63: © Chris Morphet/Redferns/Getty Images

p.64: © Chris Morphet/Redferns/Getty Images

p.65: © Chris Morphet/Redferns/Getty Images

pp.66–67: © Michael Ochs Archives/Getty Images

pp.68–69: © Ivan Keeman/Redferns/Getty Images

p.71: © Edwin Sampson / Associated Newspapers/Rex/REX USA

pp. 72–73: © Pictorial Press Ltd./Alamy

pp.74–75: © Ivan Keeman/Redferns/Getty Images

CHAPTER 9: GAMBLING ON GENIUS

pp.76–77: © K & K Ulf Kruger OHG/Redferns/Getty Images

p.78, top: © Chris Morphet/Redferns/Getty Images

p.79, top left: © David Montgomery/Getty Images

p.79, top right: © David Montgomery/Getty Images

p.79, center left: © David Montgomery/Getty Images

p.79, center right: © David Montgomery/Getty Images

p.80: © Pictorial Press Ltd./Alamy

p.81, top right: © Keystone-France/Gamma-Keystone/Getty Images

p.81, bottom right: © Associated Newspapers/Rex/REX USA

p.83: © Pictorial Press Ltd./Alamy

pp.84–85: © David Magnus/REX

p.86: © Mark and Colleen Hayward/Redferns/Getty Images

p.87, right: © Interfoto/Alamy

CHAPTER 10: THE BIG STAGE

pp.88–89: © Ivan Keeman/Redferns/Getty Images

pp.90–91: © Michael Putland/Getty Images

p.92: © Archive Photos/Getty Images

p.93: © Everett Collection/REX USA

p.94, bottom: © Peter Sanders/REX

p.95: © RB/Redferns/Getty Images

p.96: © Brian Moody/REX USA

p.97: © Ray Stevenson/REX USA

pp.98–99: © The Visualeyes Archive/Redferns/Getty Images

CHAPTER 11: TEENAGE WASTELAND

pp.100–101: © Jeffrey Mayer/WireImage/Getty Images

p.102: © Chris Morphet/Redferns/Getty Images

pp.102–103: © Chris Morphet/Redferns/Getty Images

p.104: © Chris Walter/WireImage/Getty Images

p.105, top: © David Redfern/Redferns/Getty Images

p.105, bottom: © Tony Russell/Redferns/Getty Images

p.106, bottom: © Chris Morphet/Redferns/Getty Images

p.107: © Chris Walter/WireImage/Getty Images

pp.108–109: © Ron Howard/Redferns/Getty Images

pp.110, left: © Chris Morphet/Redferns/Getty Images

p.110–111: © Jorgen Angel/Redferns/Getty Images

p.112: Ron Howard/Redferns/Getty Images

p.114: © Gijsbert Hanekroot/Redferns/Getty Images

p.115: © Jorgen Angel/Redferns/Getty Images

p.117: © Gijsbert Hanekroot/Redferns

CHAPTER 12: QUAD!

pp.118–119: © Jorgen Angel/Redferns/Getty Images

p.120, top right: © Chris Morphet/Redferns/Getty Images

p.121, top: © Michael Putland/Getty Images

p.121, bottom left: © Michael Putland/Getty Images

p.121, bottom right: © Gijsbert Hanekroot/Redferns/Getty Images

p.122, top left: © Pictorial Press Ltd./Alamy

p.123: © L. J. van Houten/REX USA

pp.124–125: © Jack Kay/Daily Express/Hulton Archive/Getty Images

p.127: © Michael Putland/Getty Images

pp.128–129: © Michael Ochs Archives/Getty Images

p.130, top: © Michael Putland/Getty Images

p.131: © Michael Putland/Getty Images

pp.132–133: © Michael Putland/Getty Images

CHAPTER 13: ROCK GODS UNDER PRESSURE

pp.134–135: © Moviestore/Rex/REX USA

p.136, top left: © David Gahr/Getty Images

p.136, bottom: © Keystone Pictures USA/Alamy

p.137, top: © Columbia Tristar/Getty Images

p.137, bottom left: © Stanley Bielecki Movie Collection/Getty Images

p.138, top left: © Anwar Hussein/WireImage/Getty Images

p.138, bottom left: © Interfoto/Alamy

p.138, bottom right: © Silver Screen Collection/Getty Images

p.139: © Pictorial Press Ltd./Alamy

p.140: © Keystone Pictures USA/Alamy

pp.141–142: © Terry O'Neill/Getty Images

p.142, bottom: © Granamour Weems Collection/Alamy

p.143, top: © David Warner Ellis/Redferns/Getty Images

p.144, bottom left: © Thorpe/Associated Newspapers/REX USA

p.145, bottom left: © Frank Edwards/Fotos International/Getty Images

pp.146–147: © Warner Brothers/Getty Images

p.148: © Gijsbert Hanekroot/Redferns/Getty Images

p.149: © Gems/Redferns/Getty Images

pp.150–151: © Trinity Mirror/Mirrorpix/Alamy

p.152, top: © James Fortune/Rex/REX USA

CHAPTER 14: BATTLING THROUGH TRAGEDY

pp.154–155: © Gijsbert Hanekroot/Redferns/Getty Images

p.156: © Monitor Picture Library/Photoshot/Getty Images

pp.156–157: © David Thorpe/REX USA

p.158, bottom left: © Bobby Bank/WireImage/Getty Images

p.159: © Michael Ochs Archives/Getty Images

p.160: © Dave Hogan/Hulton Archive/Getty Images

p.161, bottom left: © Waring Abbott/Michael Ochs Archives/Getty Images

p.162, bottom left: © John Downing/Getty Images

p.162, bottom right: © Charlyn Zlotnik/Getty Images

p.163: © Bobby Bank/WireImage/Getty Images

p.164: © David Thorpe/REX USA

p.165, bottom right: © Gary Merrin/Keystone/Getty Images

p.166: © Graham Wood / Associated Newspapers/Rex/REX USA

pp.166–167: © Associated Newspapers/Rex/REX USA

p.168: © Moviestore Collection/Rex/REX USA

p. 169, right: © Thorpe/Associated Newspapers/REX

p.170, top: © Moviestore Collection/Rex/REX USA

p.170, bottom right: © Jeremy Fletcher/Getty Images

p.171, top: © Everett Collection/REX USA

p.172: © REX USA

p.173, top: © Trinity Mirror/Mirrorpix/Alamy

CHAPTER 15: BURN OUT!

pp.174–175: © Trinity Mirror/Mirrorpix/Alamy

pp.176–177: © Martyn Goddard/REX USA

p.179, top: © Robin Anderson/REX USA

pp.180–181: © Ebet Roberts/Redferns/Getty Images

pp.182–183: © George Rose/Getty Images

p.185: © Ebet Roberts/Redferns/Getty Images

CHAPTER 16: OFF . . . AND ON

pp.186–187: © Trinity Mirror/Mirrorpix/Alamy

p.188, top left: © The LIFE Picture Collection/Getty Images

p.188, top right: © The LIFE Picture Collection/Getty Images

p.188, bottom right: © Mauro Carraro/REX USA

p.189, bottom: © Richard Young/REX USA

p.190, top: © Richard Young/REX USA

p.190, bottom left: © Phil Dent/Redferns/Getty Images

p.190, bottom right: © Associated Newspapers/Rex/REX USA

p.191, right: © Ken Towner / Associated Newspapers/Rex/REX USA

p.193: © The LIFE Picture Collection/Getty Images

p.194: © Pictorial Press Ltd./Alamy

p.195: © The LIFE Picture Collection/Getty Images

p.196: © Andre Csillag/REX USA

p.197: © Ron Galella/WireImage/Getty Images

p.198, top: © Graham Trott/Associated Newspapers/Rex/REX USA

p.198, bottom: © Ron Galella, Ltd./WireImage/Getty Images

CHAPTER 17: AND THEN THERE WERE TWO

pp.202–203: © Jeff Vinnick/Getty Images

CHAPTER 18: THE WHO REBORN

pp.208–209: © Diana Scrimgeour/Redferns/Getty Images

p.211: © KMazur/WireImage/Getty Images

p.212, top: © Bob King/Redferns/Getty Images

p.213: © dpa picture alliance archive/Alamy

p.214: © Nick Valinote/FilmMagic/Getty Images

p.215, bottom left: © Anita Bugge/WireImage/Getty Images

p.216: © SGranitz/WireImage/Getty Images

p.217, center left: © Jeff Kravitz/FilmMagic/Getty Images

p.217, bottom: © Jed Jacobsohn/Getty Images

p.218, top right: © Jamie Squire/Getty Images

p.218, bottom: © Action Plus Sports Images/Alamy

p.220, top left: © David M. Benett/Getty Images

p.220, top right: © Mick Hutson/Getty Images

p.220, bottom: © Mick Hutson/Getty Images

p.221: © Matt Kent/WireImage/Getty Images

p.223: © Brian Rasic/Getty Images

Index

Entries in *italics* indicate photographs.

ACKNOWLEDGMENTS

For the invaluable writing on the Who by Mark Blake,
Richie Unterberger, Dave Marsh, Andy Neill, Matt Kent,
Pete Townshend himself, Charles Shaar Murray, Roy Carr,
and many more over the decades, the author is profoundly grateful.

ABOUT THE AUTHOR

London-born journalist and author Mat Snow is the award-winning
former editor not only of the world-renowned music magazine *Mojo*
but also the hardly less prestigious soccer magazine *FourFourTwo*.
He has interviewed the Who, the Rolling Stones, Led Zeppelin,
Pink Floyd, the Kinks, half the Beatles, and many more, and is the
author of *U2: Revolution* (Race Point, 2014). The Who, in 1975, remains
the most exciting rock band he has ever seen. He lives in London with
a daughter named after a Kinks song, a dog named after Dolly Parton,
and a wife named Jax, but not after the New Orleans brewery.